David Cecil

David Cecil

A Portrait by his Friends

COLLECTED AND INTRODUCED BY
HANNAH CRANBORNE

DOVECOTE PRESS

First published in 1990 by The Dovecote Press Ltd
Stanbridge, Wimborne, Dorset BH21 4JD

Reprinted 1991

ISBN 0 946159 77 7

Designed by Humphrey Stone

Photoset in Sabon by Character Graphics,
Taunton, Somerset
Printed and bound in Great Britain by
Biddles Ltd, Guildford and King's Lynn

Contents

Introduction

I was lucky enough to have spent a great deal of time with David Cecil during the last ten years of his life. He always made time for conversation at which he excelled and although there was plenty of that, it never affected the speed at which he delivered his words – always flat out. This makes it difficult to re-capture his talk and yet I feel that if, with the help of his friends, we can remember something of what he was like, a kind of tapestry could be created that would serve to remind us of him. In certain contexts, certainly in academic life where writing comes more easily, his pupils will recall fluently and vividly, the lectures he delivered with such brilliance, the atmosphere at tutorials, his views, his enthusiasms, his small eccentricities; but others will recall the rest of his life, partly in anecdotes, partly in reminiscence and they are just as important a part of the whole.

Why me? I married David's great-nephew and the first people I was taken to see on coming to Cranborne were David and Rachel. We became firm friends. Later we moved to Cranborne and our friendship grew into a wonderful habit. Geography was on our side as our houses were separated by the Cranborne-Martin road. Much time, as I recall, was spent in the middle of that road. It was while living in Dorset that I got to know David and Rachel so well and where I was a partial witness to the end of a gloriously happy marriage from which David was, with great courage, to re-emerge for a final few years.

I had young children and a husband who was the newly elected Member of Parliament for South Dorset. Separated by politics for much of the time from my husband, this friendship became very important to me. I was always touched by David's friendship, amused by his company, educated by his wisdom. As a widower, a state he never got used to, David spent much of his time with us and it was always with a real tinge of sadness that I would see him enter his empty house and close his front door. He was never meant to live alone.

The most important part of David's life was his family. His children were devoted to him and there was never a night when one of them did not telephone. Their lives and commitments prevented them from spending much time with him but the telephone was always a great solace. As a widower, telephoning his children took on a new meaning. News, plans, visits, would constitute a very minor part of the conversation; lengthy discussions would take place about the part Jonathan was playing, the other actors, their lives, their problems. Then there was the world of childrens' books where his daughter Laura worked, while Hugh who was following in his footsteps, teaching, was of course always close to his heart. Nevertheless the telephone bill had to be paid, and so ashamed did David feel at this one extravagance that he would take himself off to the neighbouring town and pay it while trying to look vaguely anonymous or as if he ran a business, rather than face the shocked look of disbelief on the face of the Cranborne postmistress who knew that he did not. I don't think he realized that telephone bills could be paid by post.

So, with the advice and encouragement of David's children, I have collected some of his closest friends' and colleagues' memories of him. Many of David's friendships spanned a lifetime; however, I have tried to fit in these recollections chronologically. Inevitably they overlap, but in general I have preferred not to fragment these pieces in an attempt at cohesion. In positioning them I have been guided by the period the writer is principally concerned with.

In his book *The Cecils of Hatfield House* David tells us that he felt unequal to writing about his mother because unqualified praise was so often unconvincing. David's own children echo these feelings. Luckily they have shared with me many of their memories and the book would have been impossible without their support and encouragement. Jonathan, with his exceptional memory, provided me with many of the biographical details with which I have linked each section. The book has been very much a shared enterprise for which I would also like to thank David Burnett for his enthusiasm, his encouragement and his generous approach to this venture, and Paul Binding who helped with much of the editing. Without the help and support of my husband Robert, I would have given up at the start. He has corrected my spelling mistakes, improved my grammar, helped with the editing and put me right when I was going wrong, always encouraging and always enthusiastic. Lastly, but most important for obvious reasons, I thank David's friends and relations for so generously sending me their memories of David and for their patience and understanding.

David was very much alive until the week he died. Indeed, the last performance he gave was a month before the end when he joined the great violinist Iona Brown in a talk with music in Broadchalke church. She said afterwards 'I knew that would be our last meeting – but it was a glorious occasion and one that will stay with me forever'. All of us perhaps felt much the same way about our last meeting with David.

HANNAH CRANBORNE

Cranborne, 1990

PART ONE

1902 – 1929

1902 – 1929

D AVID CECIL was born in 1902 the fourth child and younger son of the 4th Marquess of Salisbury. He was not expected to live and remained delicate for the rest of his childhood. His parents kept him at home for longer than was usual, even in the Cecil family who distrusted schoolmasters and sent their children to school as late as possible.

David used to describe the hours he spent in the company of his mother. They did everything together, since his siblings were so much older, and as she went about her duties on the estate, either at Hatfield or at Cranborne, he would go too. He was deeply attached to her and particularly admired her practical sympathy for people who needed help. He often said that in modern times she would have been a social worker. In fact she was to remain part of his life always, for, as with Rachel after her death, he would keep her about him, talking about her not in a nostalgic way, but referring to her opinions or speculating as to what her reaction would have been to the events of the day. This was a great solace to him although he was quite unconscious of it.

When not with his mother, he would often be with his uncles and aunts, some of whom lived dotted around the house or the estate. At meal times where food had low priority and was said to be disgusting, conversation, especially with his relations, was always lively. Luckily for David he revelled in conversation, for his unusual and intelligent family made no allowances for his extreme youth. He would have to back up his opinions with good reasons.

These relations were the sons and daughters of the 3rd Marquess and included Lady Gwendolen Cecil, Lord Hugh and Lord Robert Cecil. They themselves did not refrain from expressing their opinions of David. His Uncle Nigs (Lord Edward Cecil) wrote in rather a gloomy letter 'David seems something of a firework,' implying that however brilliant he was now, he might fizzle out later. Clearly, though, David was very stimulated. Once, his mother was discussing disabilities and said how awful it must be for Aunt Nellie (Lady Robert Cecil) to be so deaf. David replied 'Yes, but think how much worse to be dumb.'

Of David's relations, the greatest influence on him was Lord Hugh, known as Linky. From him, David learnt three things. 'I learnt always to think and not to talk sloppily, to use the best words you can and I think the most important, I learnt not to have package-deal opinions.' He went on to describe a package-deal opinion as 'you think one thing and then you think something else as the same kind of people think. For instance my Uncle Hugh was not a pacifist. Indeed he rather touchingly joined the Air Force when he was nearly 40. There was nobody less fitted to it but he thought it was terrible [for someone] to be made to join the Army against their conscience, and he asked leave from the Air Force to come and make a powerful speech in the House of Commons in favour of conscientious objectors. I did learn from that to be very [suspicious of and to] dislike what I call package-deal opinions . . . that you have one group of opinions that you attach yourself to — I think [people] feel cosy with all the other package-dealers, but I don't.'

What David particularly liked about Linky was that he was not in the least intimidating, in spite of his great learning and his formidable reputation as a debater in the House of Commons. His brother Bobbety used to illustrate David and his own relationship with Linky by re-calling a walking tour the three of them took in the Dolomites in about 1920. Linky succeeded in irritating the brothers by walking very quickly. However, since he never put one foot to the ground more than six inches in front of the other he had very little progress to show for all his pedestrian activity. He irritated them all the more by arguing forcefully with them about abstruse points of theology. As a clincher to one particularly long altercation, Linky finally exclaimed: 'I suppose you will now tell me that you do not believe in the verbal inspiration of St Paul.' David and Bobbety confabulated and came to the conclusion that on the whole they did not and said so. Linky was furious and refused to speak to them for two days.

David was very fond of his father, but always remained in tremend-ous awe of him. Lord Salisbury was a busy politician and therefore could not spend as much time with David as he would have liked. But even if he had been able to do so, he did not possess the gift for easy intimacy that David himself had in such abundance. He was deeply religious and suffered from terrible crises of conscience. The dreaded melancholia never left him. Sometimes the conflict proved too much and expressed itself in dreadful fits of anger. However, his saintliness did not allow him to lose his temper and he merely quivered. This made him terrifying, especially to servants to whom he never raised his voice. This lack of intimacy must have been particularly dreadful for David as there was so much he would have liked to have discussed with his father.

David was constantly ill between the ages of 9 and 11. He had an operation for TB to take a gland out of his neck. It was successful but he did spend a great deal of time in bed. It was then that David developed his taste for the 'fine art of reading'. He read and he read and he read. He had all the time in which to do so but he never tired of it.

Soon the question of his education arose. Since he was so delicate, his parents wondered whether he should go to school at all. However, after much controversy within the family, he was sent to a neighbouring prep school for a short time. Eventually he found himself at Eton between 1915 and 1919. David was not always consistent about his time at Eton. For instance he told Isaiah Berlin that he had been very unhappy while there. 'I didn't really fit', he said, 'I was rather aesthetic and rather gentle and I don't think they liked me terribly much. I had very few friends.' A letter from A M Goodhart, David's Housemaster (see Hugh Cecil's 'My father at Eton') to his mother dated 1916 says 'His general untidiness in room and person is distressing. He is probably incorrigible on this point' and another letter in December 1917: 'David has done excellent work in some subjects and it is greatly to his credit to have done so well in the Headmaster's prize. His lapses have been due to ill health or exhaustion and it is useless to expect good results from him when he is tired – or overstrained. At the same time there is a danger of a lack of thoroughness in some of his work owing to a superficial quickness and a mind both receptive as well as mature. He is aware of this I believe, as well as his own horrible untidiness – but his sympathetic interest in discussing his own failings disarms my criticism and possibly deceives himself.' Yet towards the end of his life, David said that he had been content while at Eton though he hated being at boarding school. In his last year at school he wrote a review of Lytton Strachey's *Eminent Victorians* for an

Eton Review. It shows extraordinary maturity of style and assurance as well as how widely read he was. It was an enthusiastic article and aroused the interest of the author, so much so that he invited David to lunch in the Café Royal. This was not a success, 'Perhaps I talked too much' said David.

In 1920 David went up to Oxford. He said 'I very nearly didn't get there. I was so bad at mathematics, I failed three times in elementary mathematics to get into Oxford at all, and if I'd failed the fourth time, I would never have gone there. But I did become a Professor in the end, and it has proved to me that I think it is absolutely ridiculous to make mathematics compulsory and I cannot see why they should be, any more than music. If you can count your change that's all you have to be able to do for ordinary life.' David's health had improved but he continued to take great care of himself. He had been encouraged to do so and this habit, deeply ingrained, never left him. He never travelled without a thermometer.

He was not by nature a conventional history scholar. His talent lay rather in the imaginative perception of a period and a capacity for clear thinking. After schools he entered for the All Souls examination. He described his interview as an ignominious experience. No reassuring smiles of amused sympathy greeted him when he tripped over the carpet as he came in: his examiners remained grim throughout. Even worse, he tripped up over that same bit of carpet on his way out. It was no surprise to him that he failed to get a Fellowship. He was twenty-one.

Throughout the twenties David travelled a great deal. His brother Bobbety had been an early influence and from the first David was deeply and admiringly devoted to him. Love of music and paintings as well as poetry all originally sprang from his brother's appreciation and taste, as David's dedication in *Library Looking Glass* makes clear. Being a young man of independent means, David was able to travel. Letters he wrote to his mother, all undated, come from Portugal, France, and Italy.

In 1924 David went to Germany. These were momentous times with the struggle between the Nazis and the Communists beginning and night life in the Weimar Republic at its most decadent. But, as he was the first to confess, this nearly all passed him by. As he said himself, had he visited Sodom and Gomorrah, he would probably only have noticed the cathedral. He once said to his son Hugh that he seemed to have a gift for missing the most important events of the day. For instance, he went to Turkey with Anthony Eden from Oxford where he was invited to meet a man who was going to change the face of Turkey. He turned this opportunity down because he felt tired. The man's name was Kemal (Ataturk). In Germany this knack may have been encouraged by a lack of sympathy for the Germans, a feeling he never lost.

During his time in Germany David took lessons in the language. Through illness he was absent from his lessons for a week. When he returned, he explained to the lady teacher that he had been in bed with 'flu. She looked puzzled. 'I do not know this girl's name 'Flu'. 'Flo' I know, but not 'Flu''. She seemed in no way surprised at what seemed to her a perfectly reasonable excuse for a young man.

In 1926 David went to America with Sylvester Gates, an Oxford friend. They travelled extensively to Las Vegas, Chicago, New York, and Los Angeles where they visited David's great friend Anthony (Puffin) Asquith who was learning his trade as a film director. It was on this trip to California that they stayed at San Simeon, William Randolph Hearst's white elephant of a house. The millionaire was not there himself, and his mistress Marion Davies and her son were their hosts. David and Sylvester were commandeered for endless games of tennis where it became perfectly clear that the guests were not supposed to win. David described his amused reactions to certain facets of American life in almost indecipherable letters to his mother.

David constantly travelled to Venice where he stayed with his friend Leslie Hartley. It was like a second home and he would often bring friends out with him.

He had been elected a Fellow of Wadham College in 1924 and he spent the rest of the '20's most agreeably: travelling when he was able, writing reviews, teaching history, developing great friendships, including a very intense literary and entirely platonic relationship with Elizabeth Bowen.

It was at about this time that Constable the publishers were doing a series on the lesser known English poets and David's name came up as a brilliant young don. He had written a number of reviews in periodicals and indeed was always writing something, but Constable gave him his first opportunity to write a full biography. *The Stricken Deer*, the life of William Cowper, was published to great literary acclaim in 1929 and later won the Hawthornden Prize.

HC

[11]

Early Childhood

MARY MANNERS

The Dowager Lady Manners was one of the twin daughters of Lord William (Fish) Cecil. Lord William, second son of the Prime Minister Salisbury, was rector of Hatfield from 1888 until 1916 when he became Bishop of Exeter. During the years he and his family lived in the Rectory at Hatfield, Lord William would take his daughters up to the house every day. Lady Manners is David's only surviving contemporary who remembers him as a child. Here she describes those early days.

H E couldn't read at six. We were two years older and we couldn't read either. David had a marvellous verbal memory. His mother would read Macbeth and then David would read a scene to us. He knew that we knew that he could not read. It was thus that we started acting. He taught us the witches' scene from Macbeth. We played it up on the top floor at Hatfield, on the roundabout outside the nursery. Aunt Alice knew that he ought to be kept back. She could not resist reading to this highly sensitive, intelligent son. David had this huge head and this puny body. He never stopped talking – I remember he talked a great deal whilst sitting on his pot.

We knew all the lofts in Hatfield House. We used to go out on the leads and look at the view – quite alone. There were not many rules. We were allowed into Ellen Allen's[1] still room. Ellen Allen was Mrs Allen's sister. We were not allowed into the steward's room or the kitchen. Anything David did not like he would ignore. I remember he was given a bicycle to which he paid no attention. It was as if it did not exist. He loathed dressing and I can still see him standing while Mrs Allen dressed him. He disliked intensely being a boy and there were

1. The Allen sisters came from Northumberland and were famous characters. Isabella Allen became the young Cecils' nanny, and her sister Ellen the housekeeper. There is still a room known as 'Ellen Allen's Room' at Hatfield.

special tunics which he was allowed to wear. I don't ever remember having lessons. David had a mental uplift from being with his uncles, with whom he never stopped talking. I remember more acting, this time in the Long Gallery – promotion! – and we were playing some Oscar Wilde. During those years, David's sister Mima (Lady Harlech) would come down to Hatfield in order to unspoil him. She was eleven years older than David.

Some time later, I think David had a complete physical breakdown, which turned out to be tuberculosis. I accompanied him to Lulworth, to some lodgings where he recuperated. I don't know why it was me that went but my twin was much more reserved. I was robust, an Alderson[2] and not caring how much David talked. I remember David's bath towel getting lost. We all searched and searched and finally it was found – he was wearing it. He only survived Eton by spending a day a week in bed. David's maternal grandmother had died of TB and this was always in his mother's thoughts. He failed twice to get into Oxford because of Mathematics, only narrowly passing the third time. He was the most intelligent person I ever knew.

2. Miss Georgina Alderson married Robert Cecil, later 3rd Marquess of Salisbury, in 1857. A woman of powerful personality and intellect, her father-in-law considered her, a mere judge's daughter, of too humble an origin for his son and ostracized the young couple. Georgina Alderson was Lady Manners's and David's grandmother.

Notes on my Father's Early Childhood

LAURA HORNAK

H IS most loved toys were golliwogs. He must have got this interest
from the *Golliwog* picture books by Florence and Bertha Upton
which were his favourite stories. He invented his own country for the
golliwogs which was situated above Heaven, so the golliwogs had to
pray with their hands pointing downwards rather than upwards. His
favourite was called Miss Eileen. She was given to him as a present to
cheer him up, after the chauffeur had accidentally shut the car door
hard on his finger. He must have been about four years old. Miss Eileen was particularly splendid and became the most important character in his fantasies about the golliwog world. In one of his games she
was engaged to be married to Mr Golly. However, on the way to the
church she leapt from her carriage into the carriage of a much more
dashing golliwog, Hoffnei, and eloped with him. When my aunt Mima
asked my father why Miss Eileen preferred Hoffnei to Mr Golly, he replied, 'Because he could give her the things Miss Eileen liked.' Aunt
Mima loved this explanation and it became a family catchphrase.

His mother believed that children should be encouraged in any interest they showed. My father's interest in Shakespeare was greatly encouraged by her. She took him when he was about six years old to see
Lewis Waller as Henry V in a famous and spectacular production. His
nanny felt he was often too stimulated and this was bad for his health.
Presumably she had to cope with settling him down after an over exciting expedition. His nanny or Nana as he called her, was a very important figure in his life. She always called him by his title and if he was
naughty she would say, 'Have done, Lord David.'

Nana used to take him out to Green Park in the mornings and to
Hyde Park in the afternoons. He used to play with Lady Elizabeth
Bowes-Lyon, later Queen Elizabeth the Queen Mother. He was six and
she was slightly older. He said she was his first love.

My father started writing during his childhood and early on he was ambitious to be a writer. His first poem began: 'Oh Moon, Moon white as the table cloth.' It never got further than that first line.

When he was older he enjoyed walking round the Hatfield maze. He knew it so well he could walk round it blindfold. He also enjoyed tobogganing down the slopes of Hatfield Vineyard on a tin tray. I found it very surprising when he told me this.

His tuberculosis was the major event in his childhood. His condition was discovered almost by accident when he was seven or eight years old. His mother was taking his sister, Moucher, to the doctor and David came too. She had not thought he was ill. The doctor apparently concluded that Moucher was all right but said, 'If that was my little boy I would be very worried.' My father had an operation to remove the tubercular gland in his neck, which was performed on the nursery table at Arlington Street.[1] This was certainly a much less infectious place than a hospital.

1. 20 Arlington Street was the Salisburys' London House which was sold after the First World War when they moved into 21 Arlington Street.

A Cousin's Memories

MOLLY HOWICK

Lady Mary Howick, daughter of the 5th Earl Grey, was a cousin of David's through her grandmother Lady Selborne, elder daughter of Prime Minister Salisbury. As a child she often went to Hatfield and was much loved by her Cecil cousins. She married Sir Evelyn Baring, one of the last Colonial Pro-Consuls.

I first remember David when he was about nine, when I would be three or four. He was my mother's first cousin, and her relationship to all his family was very close. He used to come and stay at Howick with his delightful old Northumbrian Nana. I can still hear her saying in a strong local accent 'Eeh *M'Lady*' in a tone of protest when his mother had enquired if he had all he needed. In those days he would tell us stories or read to us, and when he was tired of that he would sit in an armchair immersed in a book by himself while we were taken unwillingly for nursery walks.

After that, my early memories of him all centre on Hatfield where I used to go a great deal as a girl. Sometimes there would be no one there except family (a very large one if you include all the uncles and aunts and cousins) and sometimes it would be a week-end party of all ages. At these, there were nearly always games after dinner, at which David excelled: charades, dumb crambo, clumps, talking and conversation games. And occasionally a Cotillion, which I have never met anywhere else. This was great fun, with elaborate 'figures' all designed to help young ladies to flirt and make romantic friendships. For instance, a girl sat in a chair holding a looking glass, and the men would come up behind and lean over her shoulder and look in the glass. If it wasn't the one she wanted she would scrub his face out with a duster. David's cousins, Billy and Jimmie Smith and Pauly Sudley were also brilliant at all these games and they seemed to inspire each other with infectious high spirits and imagination in inventing ingenious scenes to act. And they were all so well-read. Quotes from the poets with double meanings and historical scenes and a lot of stories from the Old Testament (which nobody seems to know now) were the sort of subjects they thought up. Another great friend was Puffin Asquith and, after David went to Oxford, Leslie Hartley. And in between the games there was endless, endless talk.

In fact, talk became increasingly David's favourite leisure pursuit. He told me that he owed a great deal to his uncle Lord Hugh Cecil – Linky as he was called – who trained him not to be slipshod in conversation. He once asked David what he would aim at in his life, and David answered 'I suppose making as many people happy as possible'; Linky was caustic in his reply: 'Any competent licensed victualler could do as well'. It was a tough school being brought up in that family.

David enjoyed young people and when he was a don he became a very good teacher. This was partly because he had a great deal of patience. These qualities and no doubt others added a spice to his own very retentive and critical mind, always full of original ideas. He said one of the best tests of whether someone was clever or not was the number of 'mental events' that happened in his mind. I am not sure if this was David's own definition or whether he was quoting his father-in-law Desmond MacCarthy for whom he had a great admiration. But it was very apt: and it certainly applied to his own mind which was full of mental events.

He was quite interesting about the ordinary daily life at Oxford. When he first became a don it was usual for them to dine in Hall nearly every night, and this resulted in a great deal of academic and general conversation between the dons and students of all ages. But gradually over the years domestic servants decreased and then began to vanish altogether, and the dons one by one got terrible consciences about leaving their wives alone in the evenings with all the cooking and the washing up for the family. This meant that fewer and fewer of them would dine in Hall at all regularly so that one of the most valuable and characteristic features of University life, intelligent conversation, in time died out in that context. Of course the quality of this kind of talk must have varied a lot over the years.

David later went so far as to say that the disappearance of domestic servants was responsible in his view for the greatest of all changes in our present way of life, even more than scientific inventions. For intelligent and stimulating talk depends upon the interchange of minds with leisure to think.

In middle age I was lucky enough to stay every year with K Elliot at North Berwick for a part of the Edinburgh Festival. Jimmie Smith, Puffin Asquith and David and Rachel completed the party, and there the talk was about music, led by Puffin but closely followed by the others. Their combined knowledge was amazing and included many uproarious anecotes about opera or performers or composers. After the house at North Berwick could no longer be used we often stayed at Harwood, near Hawick, K Elliot's home. There the conversation continued and one had the feeling that it was picked up exactly where it had been left off the year before. By that time David had retired and was no longer working quite so hard. Perhaps that gave him more time for friends and family.

It certainly gave us more opportunities to enjoy him, particularly in country house visits. There talk could range at leisure over many subjects, all enthralling. One such house was Ewelme, where Patricia Hambleden lived. She had known David intimately for years, as he had been her husband Billy's greatest friend. They shared many of the same tastes and I think David had always been a great support and counsellor after Billy died. This is one of the examples of his gift of sympathy and understanding, which so many people must have been grateful for. And of course we are all grateful for his books.

One of David's favourite themes was that we all crave perfection because we are caught up in the general human predicament of living in an imperfect world which can never satisfy us. True art, of whatever kind, can supply this need and his writing certainly does. Everything he wrote is stimulating and delightful, and full of his own very characteristic wisdom. He was a very wise man and he was deeply sensitive to other people's worries and moods, ready to laugh or cry with us all, and at the same time help us to see things in perspective. He had a marvellous sense of humour, particularly for the ridiculous, and used to say 'You must learn to laugh at nothing for there is very often nothing to laugh at,' which I think was an aphorism of his mother's.

He adored her company, and I think he especially enjoyed talking to witty and intelligent women. Cynthia Asquith and Joan Drogheda for example were special friends, and if he spotted one of them at a party he would sit on a sofa with her the whole evening regardless of anyone else. But more than any outsiders, he liked being with his own family best; brother, sisters and their children and his own, and as he got older he didn't really want any other company. Apart from anything else they entertained him so much. His daughter Laura went with him to see Coventry Cathedral and after looking silently around said 'It ought to be dedicated to St Odeon', a remark which David loved and repeated.

Of course his first love was Rachel. It was fascinating staying in a house with them and listening to the muffled sound of non-stop conversation coming from their room. One wondered if they ever went to sleep: they were certainly never silent when alone together for a moment. When asked in a television programme about his marriage, David replied 'It has been so happy that it's boring to talk about it.'

My Father at Eton

HUGH CECIL

MY father often used to talk to us of Eton, not nostalgically, but to
compare notes with our own experiences. He was ill so much as
a boy that he spent relatively little time there, which probably bene-
fited his intellectual development. He left before he was eighteen, having only reached a fairly lowly position in the school academically.
Even so, he made his mark and actually enjoyed a good deal of school
life – all the more surprising because his father, his uncles and his
grandfather detested the place.

Compared with home or with Oxford afterwards, it was of course
unimportant to him, and he was unlucky in his House, which was a
notoriously bad one. His Housemaster, Mr A. M. Goodhart, was 'a
deplorable figure – perfectly futile,' quite unable to cope with the
tougher and more rowdy senior boys, with the consequence that the
place at one time became thoroughly out of hand. One boy, Philip
Eliot, a good-looking redhaired youth, was at the centre of every kind
of racket until he was expelled in 1918. After this the moral tone began
to improve though its social attractions remained somewhat limited.
About five years after this episode a friend of my father's visited the
United States and reported that he had met a very agreeable bootlegger
out there who wished to be remembered to him. Philip Eliot had not
changed his ways.

Mr Goodhart tried to keep order by prowling about the house at
night in the hope of detecting the elusive sound of vice. One evening a
boy leant out of his room and hurled a tray at the back of the patrolling
housemaster. Goodhart, after trying in vain to locate the culprit, went
up to the next two floors, where the same thing happened, twice over.
The next morning at 6.30 am he rang the fire alarm and summoned the
boys to the pupil room 'immediately – just as you are.' Thereupon half
the house tore off their pyjamas and came down naked or wearing only
a pair of spectacles, a sock or a shoe – all of which made a farce of

Mr Goodhart's solemn interrogation. Had he lived up to his name and been a genial man, his flounderings would have inspired more sympathy in boys like my father but he came over as petty-minded and self-pitying. This was a shame, for his reports show that he thought well of my father's abilities and character.

Because of his gift for language and his endless practice at arguing at Hatfield, my father was effective at holding his own, verbally, in this bear garden. He noticed that an offensive personal remark, however irrelevant, was often the best way of fighting back. After one boy with a long, foolish sharp-ended chin had baited him insistently for minutes on end, he came out with 'your remarks, unlike your chin are utterly pointless' – with a deflating result far better than he could possibly have hoped.

His two great intellectual achievements were to get the Stratford Shakespeare Medal – which he shared with the later Cambridge scholar, George Rylands – and the Richards English Essay Prize. In spite of the fact that he missed so many weeks through ill health, he also won a Divinity prize. Otherwise his academic attainments were scanty, particularly where Maths were concerned. He did little Greek and hated Latin verses. These were made more of an ordeal for him by a much revered old classical scholar called Conybeare, who used to stroke the heads of his pupils as they worked, but turned on them irritably, if, like my father, they shied away from his sentimental attentions.

Eventually a friend, Anthony Bacon, put my father's name forward to be a member of the Library (House Prefect) when he was hardly seventeen. His election was an indicator that he was popular and that there was a shortage of responsible people. In fact though looking rather young, he was grown-up for his age mentally and confident in a way, though not typical prefect material. He remembered saying the most ridiculous things when he achieved this pinnacle of power. They struck him as absurd even as they came out of his mouth. For example, there was the standard reprimand: 'You seem to think you came to Eton to do anything you like [as though, he said, anyone in their right mind could conceivably have thought such a thing]. Well, let me tell you, you're very much mistaken.' It was in similar tones that he reduced his fag, Hugh Lygon to tears (see Anthony Powell's account), when he let his fire go out: 'You've let me down very badly, you know. I didn't expect it of you.'

Once, in the absence of the Captain, he had to beat a boy for some misdemeanour. It was a humiliating experience. He managed to strike several bits of furniture as the cane descended, so that it had slowed almost to a halt by the time it grazed the posterior of his much amused victim.

Though he felt the absurdity of school life, he was not in conscious revolt against it. He always liked games, though seldom fit enough to play; and he followed matches with great interest. He found Eton, with its complicated social customs, a fascinating laboratory for the observation of human nature in pursuit of power and glory.

Two vignettes drawn by him come to mind: One was of a boy called Hall, whose spectacular athletic performances he enjoyed watching. There was no game, seemingly, in which Hall did not excel. Yet he never achieved that coveted mark of popularity, election into 'Pop' – the Eton Society. For some reason Hall was hated. No triumph on the field could alter that. My father remembered his pale, disdainful, dissipated face, which made his star performances seem all the more exciting – it gave them a kind of evil magnificence.

The other vignette was of Michael Mason. Mason, like Hall, looked tough and contemptuous. He genuinely cared nothing for popularity, whereas Hall's sneer may have been a front. Mason later became an explorer and lived in a manor house in Oxfordshire. Members of 'Pop' in their fancy waistcoats and buttonholes used to promenade proudly arm-in-arm along a certain stretch of path in front of the school chapel – a demonstration of their importance which everyone seemed to accept – save Mason. He picked up a hose which was playing on a patch of garden nearby, and levelled it with unsmiling face, at the self-congratulatory little parade of swells. Even the fearful tanning that followed could not diminish his victory. There was nothing likeable about him, my father said, but one could only admire the courage with which he carried out this act of implacable hostility.

The war cast a gloomy shadow over the whole time he was there. Five of his first cousins were killed, not to mention a dozen more distant relations and family friends. At school, the boys had to learn a ridiculous jingle by the Headmaster, set to music by Mr Goodhart which was dedicated to Old Etonians at the Front:

> We don't forget – while in this dark December
> We sit in schoolrooms that you know so well,
> The clock, the hurrying feet, the chapel bell:

And hear the sounds that you so well remember –
Others are sitting in the seats you sat in:
There's nothing else seems altered here – and yet
Through all of it, the same old Greek and Latin
You know we don't forget.

which my father always thought was one of the flattest pieces of verse ever written.

After the Armistice, my father remembered reading the reports on the Victory Ball in late November, a jamboree for the rich which his aunts and uncles thought was in the worst possible taste, after all the suffering. Spottiswood's, the Eton bookshop, had a large lectern on which an open copy of *The Times* was spread so that the boys could read the War news. It began to be noticed that the boys were queuing up to read the paper in large numbers in the weeks after the Victory Ball. A well-known actress, Billie Carleton, had died of a drug overdose after going to it; a scandalous trial followed, culminating in the conviction of the society couturier Reggie de Veulle. Before this climactic moment, however, one of the masters intervened to save the boys from moral corruption. Spottiswood's were asked to remove their copy of *The Times*.

Apart from Anthony Bacon, my father's closest friends were Bob Gathorne-Hardy (also in Goodhart's) and Eddy Sackville-West, both already fully-fledged aesthetes, with whom he was able to spend time on a high-brow – though frivolous – plane, during his later years at school.

While still at Eton, he spent a few weeks with his brother Bobbety who was working as an assistant to their Uncle Bob at the Paris Peace Conference. Eddy Sackville-West, whose father was also at the Conference, went over to Paris with him. My father left Eton at the end of 1919. He was keen to do so, and it was generally felt that staying on would do little to advance his education before he went on to Oxford.

Adolescence

DIANA GAGE

*The Dowager Viscountess Gage was born Diana Cavendish and
was the daughter of Lord Richard and Lady Moyra Cavendish.
Her elder sister Betty married David's brother Bobbety,
the 5th Marquess of Salisbury.*

IT was in 1915 that I first met David. The start of a long friendship. I
remember his pale sensitive face, talkativeness, expressive, gestic-
ulating, delicate hands and especially his kindness to a shy quiet six
year old.

The event was the marriage of his brother Bobbety to my sister
Betty.

I drove to the church in a brougham in the company of my mother
and Lady Astor and can clearly recall Lady Astor saying several times
'this is not a romantic marriage, both families want it'.

There were one or two hitches. Mary Cavendish, a bridesmaid to-
be, was concussed, and a fat cousin squeezed into her dress. The
Bishop's crozier was mislaid. It had arrived in a flat case and was taken
into the gunroom. The youth of the bride and groom, uniforms
everywhere, a vivid reminder of the war, made for an exceptionally
emotional atmosphere. This was not apparent in the nursery, but
David told me later how charged it was and how he gave brandy to the
most distressed and calmed and encouraged others.

I think he always enjoyed the role of an involved spectator.

He must have been fifteen at the time and later he told of being asked
at the last moment to a dinner party given by Lady Desborough. He
had known her all his life but was alarmed by this occasion. She placed
him at her left hand. They both had the ability to bring out the best in
everyone, and an immense capacity for enjoyment. When she turned to
talk to him all trepidation vanished into an evening of pure pleasure.

Another time David and his parents were staying at Holker for

[24]

Christmas and New Year. We did not go out at all, and ignored the dark cold days in the delight his company provided indoors. Suddenly there was a moment of the feeling of the turn of the year and I can remember David, quite still, enjoying the soft lights of the winter sky. He loved people and life, but I think his greatest affinity was with quiet lives and scenes.

I have photographs of him cooking at picnics, paddling in Windermere, cockling in Morecambe Bay. Not the activities one would associate with him, but perhaps he felt he should take the part of the ideal guest and enjoy what was offered.

He was best of all at Hatfield, which he loved, making one share in the interest and beauty of the house and those who had lived there.

Lady Gwendolen Cecil wrote: 'As in all families who are not entirely frivolous, the conversation was mainly of politics and the church'. She and her brothers used to pace up and down the long gallery discussing and arguing. They were high minded, serious but also quick and amusing – and interested in new ideas, even when presented by the very young. When David joined them it seemed the repartee was faster and the laughter more frequent.

Once while talking of Lord Melbourne, the subject switched to Lord Byron and his relationship with Augusta – obviously of interest to the more austere older generation.

Cotillions were a fashion in the twenties. There were various figures and people gave each other presents and favours. Two leaders were needed to give pace and direction and David and his sister Moucher were in much request as such.

He was genuinely vague. Once I had an urgent call for the return of a book he had lent, as he had written a draft for part of the Stricken Deer on the fly leaves. But sometimes he turned this absence of mind to good account to avoid an unwelcome engagement.

Thoughtful and considerate of everyone but capable of criticism, which he would guiltily atone for by remembering their good qualities.

A robust romantic, he endowed his friends with every desirable quality and gave an added zest to living.

A Cranborne Neighbour

ALBERT PETTIS

*The Pettis family moved to Cranborne at the turn of the century.
Albert Pettis was born in 1902, and therefore was exactly the
same age as David. In 1918, his mother heard there was a job
as hallboy at Hatfield and applied on his behalf. He got the
job and within three months was promoted
to 3rd footman.*

I was 16, the same age as Lord David. I was made third footman. The
third footman would look after the youngest one in the family and
that was Lord David. He was smart – always smarter than Lord
Bobbety as we called him – His mother used to buy him the clothes that
he wanted.

He wasn't sporty and he didn't like shooting. He used to spend a lot
of time with his books. I remember several times though when we
played golf. Once, he asked me to play I said that I was on duty and
couldn't. Lord David said 'Pettis, I'll arrange it.' He spoke to Mr
Couzins, the Steward and I was allowed off. That was when there was
a golf course in the park. Neither of us could play I remember – and we
lost quite a few balls.

We were like brothers. He always gave me a birthday present.

Lord David used to walk up through Cranborne with Sir John
Betjeman having a good old conversation – hair flowing in the wind –
they'd stop, hands would wave and they would then go on a little
further, still talking. My wife said 'Who's that?' I said that's Lord
David with Sir John Betjeman 'Oh aren't I pleased I've seen them' she
said.

Lord David was often in the middle of the road. I remember the bus
driver saying 'Who's that bloody old man always in the middle of the
road. One day I shall knock him over'.

After Lady David died, Lord David said 'I can't get over the loneliness'. When my wife died he said to me 'I'd like you to come to tea. Now you know what it is like being lonely'. We commiserated with each other.

An Early Friendship

ANTHONY POWELL

Anthony Powell CH, *novelist and Eton
contemporary, remained a friend of David's
for the rest of his life.*

D AVID Cecil, as a boy of sixteen or seventeen, was quite absurdly
like himself as a distinguished man of letters in his eighties. There
was scarcely any difference. I can think of no one whose manner and
appearance were less changed by time, though latterly he would
sometimes have a front tooth missing, which gave a slightly piratical
air. No doubt that would have been equally true at the moment when
one loses the teeth of childhood, but that was before I knew him.

My second or third half at Eton I was David's fag. He was only high
enough up in the house (Goodhart's) to have one fag (senior boys had
two or three), so that what little there was to be done devolved on me.
It was a winter half. One of the fag's jobs was to keep an eye on his
fagmaster's fire, though he did not have to lay it.

One evening an odious boy called Sewell sought me out. 'You're in
for it,' he said. 'You've let Cecil's fire out.' I don't think it was any of
his business, at the same time it was just as well to know this disaster
had taken place.

Goodhart's was an extremely easy-going house, but reasonable
exception might be taken by the least exacting to this dereliction of
duty. It is now obscure to me why I did not simply remake the fire.
Probably because all the kindling had been burned, no more available
from any source one knew of. I thought the best thing would be to
make an immediate confession. I found David. 'I'm afraid I've let your
fire out, Cecil' I said.

David was charming. He replied: 'That's all right. It isn't
particularly cold tonight.' Anyway some remark that amounted to
that.

When only a few years ago we were lunching at Red Lion House, Cranborne, David was talking about Eton. It was a period in his life which he described as 'perfectly tolerable.' I reminded him of the fire incident. David said: 'The previous winter half Hugh Lygon had been my fag. He, too, let the fire out. I did rather scold him. Then a huge tear trembled in one of his eyes, and rolled down his cheek. I felt awful.' Nonetheless, this earlier failing to keep a fire in would have been an understandable reason to have been more, rather than less, forbearing when that happened again.

David had gone down from Oxford, I think, before I came up, not yet become a don. He had belonged to the last Oxford generation to sustain a small set of quiet, well behaved, smartish, reasonably intelligent undergraduates (as opposed to the horsey, golfing Bullingdon) with a social life of its own. These (slightly overlapping each way) fitted in between those who had been 'in the war', and the rackety crowd (largely associated with the Hypocrites Club[1]), which made much of the going just before, and during the early part, of my own Oxford residence.

While I was up I met David at least once with Lady Ottoline Morrell at Garsington Manor. I remember him there with his lifelong friend Leslie Hartley. I don't think any sort of recognition took place between us on any Garsington occasion. The atmosphere, the least socially easy in the world, would have discouraged anything in the shape of schooldays' reminiscence. Nonetheless, Lady Ottoline's ominous, husky, hissing pronouncements on life and art, uttered as if through the nose, did nothing to stem David's rapid breathless flow of words, notably individual phrases.

Later in London, when I used to read David's literary criticism now and again, his views seemed old fashioned, not to say stuffy, to a degree. Now I see there was much to be said for the stand he took about Scott, George Eliot, Hardy, in fact the Victorians in general. It was a hard thing to do at that moment. David remained always worth hearing on writers he liked. For those he cared for less he usually preferred to remain on the safe side, rather than indulge in controversy. For example, he possessed no great taste for Conrad,but would be unwilling to defend an anti-Conrad position.

David had long known the Pakenham family, and when I married

1 The Hypocrites was a drinking club whose members were very different from David's circle.

Violet Pakenham we became friends. I had met Rachel MacCarthy once or twice before she married David, but did not know her at all well. Violet and I lunched with David and Rachel not long after we were married. It was at the MacCarthy house in Chelsea, which the Cecils had been lent. The other guests were Cyril Connolly and his first (American) wife Jeanie.

Not long after, Violet and I attended a cocktail party at the Connollys' King's Road flat. We left at the same moment as David and Rachel. Rachel was wearing a large cartwheel hat, which suddenly blew off, sailing along the King's Road like a ship. Both David and Rachel went in pursuit. It was an hilarious scene. An on-coming bus-driver collapsed into helpless fits of laughter, taking his hands from the wheel. Later their sons Jonathan and Hugh were at Francis Cruso's house at Eton, where our own sons, Tristram and John, also boarded. John was, in fact, Hugh's fag. David was always agreeable about my books, usually writing a fan letter but it was when he gave up his Oxford job and moved to Dorset that I knew him best.

It is possible to think of David as rather a lightweight figure chattering away, apt to cut appointments, not over-good at returning books he had been lent. Indeed, that was perhaps a somewhat frequent estimate. It was not, I think, a just one. I remember having to give some sort of a talk at Oxford over which David presided, and, purely professionally, I was impressed by his firm handling of undergraduates male and female.

A story he told me a few years ago is also worth preserving to illustrate his firmer side. David recalled that early in their married life he and Rachel had dined with Alice Astor (then von Hoffmansthal), among other guests being Eve Curie (very pretty daughter of the 'radium' Curies) the French dramatist Henry Bernstein (with whom Eve Curie was living), and Tom Mitford. I think I met Tom Mitford only once, then very briefly. He had the reputation of being a professionally bad-mannered man. David prefaced the story by saying he had always detested him.

Mitford sat between Eve Curie and Rachel. 'During dinner', said David, 'he did not address one single word to Rachel. Not one. He talked to Eve Curie from the beginning of the meal to the end. I was so furious about this that after dinner I at once made for Eve Curie, and monopolized her for the rest of the evening, in fact until she and Bernstein left, making sure that Tom Mitford did not get near her once.' This tougher side of David was not always appreciated.

David also played an active part in rescuing Leslie Hartley at the end of Leslie's life, from difficulties with a sinister man-servant.

A word should also be said about his extremely courageous behaviour after Rachel died. That can only have been a most appalling blow.

Nevertheless, life continued at Red Lion House under a regime of housekeepers, some more satisfactory than others. As in former days friends would be invited to luncheon, David always in his old form.

Rachel had been seriously ill for many months when David woke in the night to find that the end had come. It is said he was holding her hand. One could not help thinking of the last lines of Larkin's poem *An Arundel Tomb* with its stone figures holding hands:

> Our almost-instinct almost true:
> What will survive of us is love.

The Undergraduate

RALPH RICKETTS

*Ralph Ricketts, author and contemporary of David's at Oxford.
They did not remeet for many years, but became close
friends after Leslie Hartley's death in 1972.*

To write a satisfying description of David Cecil is like trying to paint a dragonfly on the wing!

Paul Sudley, known to his family and friends as 'Pauly', was a friend of mine at Winchester. When we found we were going up to Oxford on the same day, he to New College, I to Magdalen, we arranged to meet at the Clarendon Hotel for dinner. I arrived late to glimpse Pauly in the dining room sitting with two young men I did not know. Pauly introduced them as his cousins: Billy Smith and David Cecil. I was struck by their immediate friendliness; not for a moment did I feel an intruder in a family group.

David had come up to Oxford a term or two before Pauly, Billy and myself. He had collected a group of friends to whom he introduced us. We joined them, going about in a group, David never silent nor still. He would race up and down College staircases, his own or a friend's, dart up the High Street followed by a breathless group, jump on and off buses, glancing at a chance looking glass which might show his reflection (he had romantic looks, might have been Lord Byron's younger brother). He was always in high spirits, in love with Oxford, his friends, himself, life . . . He would throw his whole self into whatever he was doing, were it a visit to the cinema – we often went to the cinema – or a paper game in his rooms.

I don't think David had much time for intimacy in those days, except with his cousin Billy to whom he had always been attached. A man with whom he had a friendship which might be called intimate was L. P. Hartley, who was already beginning to make his name as an author of short stories, later, of course, a first rate novelist. He was some seven or eight years older than the rest of us, having served in the war before going up to Balliol. He and David had periodical lunches alone together in the Gridiron Club, known as the 'Grid'. On these days a whisper would percolate the group: 'David is having lunch with Leslie Hartley today', the implication being that they must not be disturbed.

Soon Pauly and I moved out of our respective Colleges, taking 'rooms' together. David remained in Christ Church ('The House'). I was told that the group to which I belonged was known as 'The Regiment'. If so, David must have been cast as the Colonel, which would have amused him hugely. Anyone less like the conventional image of a Colonel I cannot conceive. Gradually, though, I became disillusioned with this group with its increasing tendency to mutual admiration, but I never resigned from it. I went to delightful parties at Greenlands, the house near the river where Billy's parents lived. I also remember happily a 'Reading Party' at Moretonhampstead Manor on Dartmoor which also belonged to the Hambledens. The 'Party' consisted of Billy, David, Bob Gathorne-Hardy, a friend of David's from Eton days, Pauly, Teddy Hogg, Eardley Knollys and myself. We had three weeks of perfect summer weather. Some of us slept out of doors. I remember that we played a lot of tennis of which David was very fond. He did not care for other outdoor games or sports. Horses bored him, he was not a good shot. Indeed when asked if he liked shooting, he replied: 'I only shot once, and that was Edward Rhys in the foot.'

David was no chameleon, but he could adapt himself adroitly and with charm. He was also adept at discouraging bores who tried to presume on a superficial acquaintanceship. Without being rude he arranged it so they ceased to exist. I saw this happen several times, and was much amused.

Women Friends – A Political Friend

KATHARINE ELLIOT

*Baroness Elliot of Harwood was the daughter of Sir Charles
Tennant, the first Lord Glenconner and his second wife
Marguerite Miles. Although a Liberal by upbringing, she married
a Conservative politician, Colonel Walter Elliot, and herself
became a prominent Conservative. Harold Macmillan made her
one of his first Life Peers in 1958. David was an intimate
friend of Anthony (Puffin) Asquith one of the pioneer directors
of British films. She was his aunt, but also his contemporary,
and remembers those days in their youth. Lady Elliot was a lifelong friend of both David and Rachel and they always enjoyed
their visits to her house in the Scottish borders.*

D AVID and Puffin both loved literature and music and were the best
talkers in general conversation I have ever known. Margot
Asquith (my half sister and the Prime Minister's second wife) had a
house not far from Oxford called 'The Wharf', at Sutton Courtenay.
She was a marvellous hostess and every weekend Oxford undergraduates used to come over. We played lawn tennis, bathed in a
backwater of the Thames and always we talked incessantly. We played
cards and quiz games and occasionally acted charades. Racing Demon
was a favourite at which both Puffin and David excelled.

Desmond and Molly MacCarthy used to come down for
weekends bringing Rachel who was then in her teens. Desmond was
a marvellous conversationalist and we used to listen carefully to his
discussions with Henry Asquith on books and topical biographies.
Leslie Hartley was another visitor who came quite often and was a
great friend of David's.

I remember the excitement when Leslie's first book was published.
Maurice Bowra, a don at Oxford and a little older than David, was
another good talker. Eddy Sackville-West used to play the piano and
Jelly D'Aranyi, the great violinist, would come down and stay and we

used to have the most wonderful musical evenings. David was a listener not a performer. He loved music as we all did. About that time Puffin gave a luncheon party in his rooms at Oxford. He invited his friends to meet his 'aunt' and instead of the middle-aged lady they had been expecting to see, it was just me, the same age as his other guests. During those years, Leslie Hartley had an apartment in Venice and David used to go and stay with him. I went out with both David and Leslie in 1927, my first visit to Italy, and I shall never forget exploring the canals and being taken out in a gondola. David was extremely knowledgeable about Venetian history and I remember him giving me fascinating talks about this.

David invited me to a ball at Hatfield, what was known as a 'cotill-ion'. I had never stayed at Hatfield and was fascinated by the house with all its historic connections. Through David's mother, Lady Salis-bury, I met all the most interesting people, Lord Hugh Cecil, Lord Robert Cecil and David's brother Bobbety Cranborne. It was ex-tremely friendly and everyone talked continously, and even if one did not play an active part it was nonetheless fascinating. Being a close relation of the Asquiths I was an enthusiastic Liberal in those days and this was absolutely accepted.

When Puffin left Oxford he went into the cinema business (long before talking films) and as he became more successful, we would go with David and other friends to the first night performances of his films.

After the war ended, life returned to more normal activities. I owned a family house at North Berwick called Glenconner. I used to have special parties for the Edinburgh Festival and living so close it was easy to motor into Edinburgh to the theatre, the opera and to concerts. David and Rachel came many times as did Puffin, my sister Nancy Crathorne and my brother Peter Lubbock. We were all great en-thusiasts of The Festival to which companies from Berlin, Glyn-debourne and Covent Garden came as well as many of the great musicians. The Edinburgh Festival is now well established and has been for many years but we were some of its earliest supporters.

My husband died in 1958 and I became a Life peer which is almost a full-time occupation, but I went down to Cranborne and stayed with David and Rachel once or twice. Although we were all so much older, we still had many interests in common and many lovely memories. I was sad when Rachel died and I saw David rarely after that. His memory is ever with me, we were devoted friends and I am the proud possessor of all the books he wrote and which he kindly sent to me. No one in my generation has made a greater contribution to literature and spread his talents and his charm to more university undergraduates or to such a wide variety of people who knew and loved him. There were no dull moments in his company and I shall remember him always.

Women Friends – A Family Friend

PATRICIA HAMBLEDEN

*The Dowager Viscountess Hambleden is the daughter of the
15th Earl of Pembroke. She married the 3rd Viscount Hambleden
in 1928. Her husband 'Billy' was David's first cousin: his mother
Lady Esther Gore was the daughter of the 5th Earl of Arran and
sister of David's mother. David was always close to the
Smith family and after Billy died, he continued to see a great
deal of his widow and his brother Jimmy Smith.*

THE first time I met David was at a house party. I was 18 and
delighted to find David amongst the young. I felt I had known him
always; in fact I really got to know him after I married, as my husband
and David were not only cousins but **real** friends. I remember my
husband Billy telling me of the time he and David shared a wagon-lit:
David was on the top bunk endlessly writing whilst throwing all the
sheets of paper on the floor, which in due course Billy would pick up.
Billy would recount tales of Oxford days – talking late into the night.
David, standing with a glass in one hand, would, on occasion, be
teased by Billy who would replace his empty glass with a poker – so
absorbed with their discussion was David that he didn't notice.

Looking back, one of the things I remember most clearly about
David was the enormous interest he took in whatever one said – the
most trivial remarks were greeted with enthusiasm and interest.
Sometimes lively and even controversial discussions would ensue all
resulting from this trivial or idiotic remark. This was his gift. He was at
ease with anyone from 5 to 95 and always he made that person feel
they were much cleverer than they were.

A happier marriage than his to Rachel one could not have imagined.
I remember David at his wedding reception in Charles Street when he
kissed all his ex-girlfriends, Rachel included, before he leapt into the
car much to everyone's, including his mother's, great amusement.

Time meant nothing to David. I remember once when Rachel was not at all well and the doctor said that this was due to lack of sleep. She was forced to admit that this was because her husband would talk most of the night.

Being the youngest of his family by many years, he spent much of his holidays with his cousins the Smiths, both at Greenlands and in Devonshire. The whole of my husband's family adored him. David was very good at after dinner games and his contributions made them considerably more amusing. In telling all these fascinating and funny stories about people, I cannot recall him ever being malicious or unkind. He had a prodigious memory and would regale one with endless anecdotes.

After my husband died in 1947, David continued to come and stay and it was wonderful to talk about old times together. He and Rachel were endlessly kind to me and all of my children. He was immensely appreciative of the countryside and dearly loved Dorset, both at Rockbourne and at Cranborne. Neither he nor Rachel were gardeners but they were most appreciative of other people's gardens. One of my grandchildren, Charles Brand, who was at school nearby, was invited over to Red Lion House several times. He vividly remembers these outings and how enchanted he was by his conversations with David.

An Early Pupil

HENRY PHELPS BROWN

*Sir Henry Phelps Brown was tutored by David when he first
begin teaching at Wadham. David liked him very much as a pupil
and was impressed by his intellectual maturity. He said
it was like teaching another don.*

THISTLEDOWN, someone said – for there was a slightness and
fragility about his person that made us wonder whether one of the
gusts that hurtle through the lodge might not overturn him when he
met it at the corner, on his way from his rooms on no. 1 staircase. He
was young then, and his features called to mind a boy looking up,
fresh, eager and vulnerable, from a lowly seat in some stately family
portrait. There is a drawing by Henry Lamb, reproduced as the
frontispiece of *Library Looking-Glass* that shows him as his pupils of
those years remember him – the eyes of a poet looking far away, the
narrow-ridged nose, the full and mobile lips. When he spoke, his face
was animated by the spontaneity that brought his words out in short
rushes.

He had been elected into Fellowship on the same day as Keeley, at
the St Nicholas meeting of 1924; after a time abroad he came into
residence in Michaelmas Term the next year, to teach modern history.
What was it like to be taught by him? – the time that passed so quickly
was not to be thought of as a tutorial hour. No tutor could be less
magisterial. What he thought he put forward to the most callow youth
as though inviting his opinion on it, and the invitation was real. It was
this friendliness of his, as much as his wit, that made him outstanding
as a conversationalist. There are some who talk so well that they
deserve their Boswell, but they look more for appreciation than for
response; for Cecil conversation always meant a meeting of minds. He
looked for response, and because his interest was unforced, he
obtained it. Those who talked with him caught the spark, and began

[39]

to feel that they too were talking well. So it was with his pupils. He conveyed to them a conception of the past that was fresh and immediate, as though he had gained it (as in part he had) in talk at the family table. He was interested above all in personality. When he spoke about the politics of the past century, it was as though the stiff figures in some faded photograph had suddenly come to life and begun to move and speak. When one came down into the quad after an hour with him, to meet Peel or Palmerston walking there would not have seemed remarkable.

But though he taught history so well in his own imaginative way, and it was in the History School that he had taken his First, he must have felt increasingly that his own bent was for letters. The paper he read to the college Literary Society – it was a hilarious evening – was on 'Bad poems by good poets'. When in 1928 Russell Bretherton was elected into Fellowship it was arranged that he should take over some of the teaching of history so that Cecil might give more time to English. The next year Cecil published his *Stricken Deer*, and the acclaim with which it was received – it was awarded the Hawthornden Prize – may well have encouraged him to devote himself to letters entirely. In 1930 he gave up his Fellowship to do this.

How much he found himself at home in the College in those four or five years is hard to tell. The SCR when he joined it was what now seems incredibly small – besides the Warden, and the 'Prof' who continued to live in Christ Church, there were only six Fellows, of whom Bowra was the most junior. There was wit and to spare when Wade-Gery, Bowra and Cecil joined with undergraduates in the college Book Club, auctioning old books and deciding what new ones to order. But there must have been evenings when the Common Room seemed confined. The *Gazette* states that Cecil played hockey for the College, but that agrees so little with memories of his erratic if supple movements that, like the earlier record of Sir Thomas Beecham having represented the College at soccer, this seems a case in which the historian may prefer his vision to his documents. More persuasively the *Gazette* also states that Cecil joined with Keeley in installing new lighting in the hall.

The pencil with which this sketch has been drawn from undergraduate memory may have been biassed by the undergraduate game of exaggerating the foibles of the dons. It still would seem unnatural to write in staid terms about one who was himself so lively. But there was nothing shallow about his liveliness. The impression this memoir leaves would be one-sided if it did not make clear the standards, the strengths of purpose and the firmness of judgement that were evident to those who knew him then. We can say of him what he said of Pater, that 'he combined the two qualities essential for critical appreciation: common sense and uncommon sensibility.' His creative energy and his craftsmanship were manifest already in his study of Cowper. There was also an underlying sense of commitment and vocation. It was clear, too, when discussion neared a moral issue, that there were principles he held firmly, and that they were based on a religious faith. But this without 'high seriousness': he made no apology for enjoyment. 'I cannot recall a time,' he wrote in the preface to his personal anthology, 'when stories and rhymes and pictures and tunes were not for me the chief source of interest and pleasure in life. I stress the word pleasure. Pleasure has played a large part in my life; pleasure, solitary or sociable, carnal or spiritual, pleasure in the beauties of art and nature, in the enthralling variety of the human scene, and pleasure in jokes'. It was his gift to impart that pleasure to others.

PART TWO

1930 – 1939

1930 – 1939

WHEN David first met Rachel he was already friends with her father Desmond MacCarthy, the eminent literary critic. The MacCarthys were a very close family but at that time their relations were not at their most harmonious. Unknown to David, there were bitter quarrels between Desmond and his wife over money and over his affair with an American lady artist. Barely 20, Rachel was unsettled by this, deeply devoted as she was to both her parents. Although she had many admirers, it was towards David she inclined, feeling a real compatibility and strength. It was nearly three years before he fully understood what their feelings were for each other. Early on in their friendship, Lady Salisbury recognized that Rachel was the right person for him. 'Have you seen that nice Miss MacCarthy lately?' his mother would say, probably when he had brought somebody home to stay who pleased her less.

Although Rachel longed to marry David, so precious was this friendship and compatibility, that she was prepared to settle for that alone. Finally when David realized the nature of her feelings and that he risked losing her to somebody else, he rushed precipitately back from abroad straight to Wellington Square where he proposed to her.

The wedding took place in October 1932 in the medieval church of St Bartholomew's Smithfield. Mary Clive describes the scene: 'Rachel had no bridesmaids and looked very small and touching, rather like a child dressed up as a bride. Her going-away outfit was grey – not her colour really but I imagine it represented sophistication and romance to her. The only unusual incident in the service was that photographers crept up the aisle and photographed the bridal pair in front of the altar. The wedding presents were put on show at a reception at the Salisburys' house in Arlington Street on the morning before the wedding and the scene sticks in my memory because there were such a lot of presents and they were so recherché – their friends seemed to have taken real trouble to choose something special. There was a caricature of Max Beerbohm by himself 'distracted, thinking of a suitable wedding present'.

Then there is an account in Virginia Woolf's diaries of Rachel going up the aisle: 'It was an odd sight – Desmond with Rachel on his arm. Everybody stood up. The white and red procession with the cross in front went ahead. Then very small, smooth, pale and sleek appeared Rachel and Demond arm in arm. I have never seen him as a father. Now he was that – leading his daughter. She was a waxwork – with her diamond cross; very pale; very small; carrying a white book.' Then later: 'Then a sort of inner play went forward behind glass doors. One saw Salisburys and MacCs signing books. Then a dribble back of relatives. Then the Wagner wedding march. Then David and Rachel arm in arm sleep-walking down the aisle preceded by a cross which ushered them into a car and so into a happy long life, I make no doubt...'

David gave up his job at Wadham in 1930 as he had decided to devote himself to full time writing. He owned a house in Edwardes Square. Although he enjoyed doing up the house which had pink curtains and yellow walls, he just could not manage bachelor life. In fact whenever he was ill, he used to return to Arlington Street, his parents' house. David had a cook and butler who cheated him. Virginia Woolf's remark about there not being enough food in David's house was perfectly true for this reason. There were drawers of uncashed cheques. When Rachel found this evidence of David's complete inability to cope, she took over the accounts and all matters of a financial nature and continued to do so for the rest of her life.

After he and Rachel married, they both decided they wanted to live in the country. David sold Edwardes Square and they went to live in Rockbourne, a small village on the borders of Hampshire and Dorset, not far from his beloved Cranborne. A quiet time was needed for writing. There were quite a few friends living locally and others would come and stay. These included Cecil Beaton, the Lambs, the Johns, Leslie Hartley, Rachel's cousin Clare, and Sydney Sheppard, David's niece Mary Campbell, Puffin Asquith, the Hambledens. David's great friend Rex Whistler stayed and so did Elizabeth Bowen. His brother Bobbety lived close by at Cranborne.

David published *Sir Walter Scott* in 1933, *Early Victorian Novelists* in 1934 and *The Young Melbourne* in 1939.

In July 1937 Rex Whistler went down to Rockbourne to stay for Cecil Beaton's famous fancy dress party. When Laurie Whistler was writing the life of his brother, David sent him a collection of his own memories of his friend Rex, an extract of which describes the preparations:

He was staying with Rachel and me, and we had all been told to come dressed up as something rural. Rachel and Zita James, our other lady, had of course got their own dresses. But Rex and I had not wanted to get anything special and had agreed to get ourselves up as Victorian sportsmen with the help of what clothes we had got. But he arrived from London with some splendid additions in the way of whiskers and spats and cravats. He put all his skill as a stage designer at our disposal: I put myself in his hands; after an hour we emerged together and, I think I can say without vanity we had two of the best costumes at the party, because like everything of the kind that Rex did, they were not exaggerated and showed such a delicate sense of period that he really knew how to make one look like one of Millais' illustrations of Trollope.

Both Rachel and David longed to start a family. During the seven years before Jonathan was born, Rachel suffered agonies and doubts that perhaps she was unable to have children. She never confided in David about these worries and David later always regretted her reticence. In 1937 Rachel had a miscarriage which, though a terrible disappointment, was nevertheless a relief, as she now knew that she was able to have children.

After 7 years as a writer, David realized that he missed teaching. He was invited to put his name forward as an English Fellow at New College and was successful.

In the summer of 1938 David and Isaiah Berlin met at Bowenscourt staying with their mutual friend Elizabeth Bowen. They were both going to be dons at New College that autumn. Isaiah Berlin recalls: 'According to David, H A L Fisher, who was the Warden, said that the Common Room was so boring we were going to be the two bright young men whom he imported in order to communicate some life into it.' Talking of David and their early friendship, Isaiah Berlin said 'We got on extremely well; I thought he was wonderful; the most agreeable, intelligent charming man I had met in my life. We did talk a great deal and with Elizabeth Bowen. Three was company, oddly enough'.

In the autumn of that year David arrived at New College without Rachel who remained in Rockbourne. Again Isaiah Berlin recalls: 'We both lived in New College. We used to see each other every day, and we talked for about eight hours every day. Endlessly. He used to come and see me in the morning. He said "Not many people like being called on in the morning, but I do." He used to come after dinner having dined on the horrible New College food and then we would talk till two in the morning. We talked about people and books and music, mainly people; autobiographical details about his life, who he liked and who he didn't, why. He was a very sharp delineator of character. His vignettes were absolutely wonderful.'

In February 1939 David and Rachel's son Jonathan was born. They moved into a pretty little house in the High Street opposite Magdalen. In a letter to his mother describing the house, David refers to the pink and yellow drawing room. The colours are the same as those he had in his house in Edwardes Square. David enjoyed 'doing up' houses and he took endless trouble choosing colours and materials. This was his department, as financial matters were Rachel's domain.

In a letter to her mother-in-law, Rachel wrote: 'David is of course at Oxford this week. He gave me a detailed description over the telephone, of exactly where all the furniture has been arranged. The move went without a hitch, and everything went in without the windows being taken out.

David is most excited about doing the house. He says we have collected, thanks to you, and to Hatfield, plenty of furniture – in fact it almost looks crowded. David said, quite seriously, in a worried voice, that we must have very bright sofa and chair covers to counteract the yellow walls and pink paint as he says they make one feel "a little giddy and rather sick." I burst out laughing as really I can imagine nothing worse than having to live in such a room if it is truly the case. I am sure it will tone down – and I thought it a very good yellow – if a little too strong. It feels extraordinary not being able to be there and to be buying everything by post. Kitchen chairs, beds, and nursery things etc. I hope I shan't get a shock when I get there and find everything wrong but David was very encouraging. I am going to go for the day next Tuesday with David, on his way back. I can just manage it by giving Jonathan a bottle at two o'clock. Then next week we are all going to move which is very exciting.'

In September war was declared. David was only 37 at the outbreak of war but his health precluded him from joining up. He decided to remain in Oxford where he continued to teach throughout the war. Teaching was of course a reserved occupation. The public were 'therefore spared my services as a food controller in Fordingbridge' he said.

HC

[48]

The Engagement

A LETTER TO CYNTHIA ASQUITH
FROM DESMOND MACCARTHY
AUGUST 20TH 1932

I KNEW you would be pleased and understand how very glad I am that
Rachel has her heart's desire. You were a great comfort to me when
I worried about her possible – probable disappointment. You were
my chief confident (sic?) and it would have been through you that I
would have tried to disentangle her – at the cost of I'm afraid deep
pain had it been or seemed necessary. On the whole I thought it likely
that she would have to go without David. But for once my undecisive
character ruled me well. So delightful a thing has not happend to me
for a long time as their engagement. I know you are pleased too. I
am thankful you think R – well, what it is good to be and the sort
of girl it is natural for David to love. I do – though I know half of
her failings which perhaps you don't. I don't know any of David's. I
only feel sure of him and like him and admire him. And of course I
am very pleased too that she should become one of a family for whom
I have so much respect. I am a little embarrassed by the idea of the
actual wedding – but that's a trifle. I think I am the most fortunate
of fathers-in-law. I am a little intimidated by the idea of Hatfield,
which is a far cry from Wellington Square, but I'm not such a goose
as not to rejoice that it should be part of the background of Rachel's
life. I think she and David are suited to each other.

I must tell you how I heard the news. I was coming home jaded on
that hot Tuesday night, to dine at home. The drawing room window
was open and I saw to my surprise David and Rachel were sitting on
the sofa. I said to David 'I am surprised to see you. I thought you
were in Italy.' and he said 'Yes I was and I've another surprise for
you. I'm going to marry Rachel'. I expect I showed even more joy
than amazement. Dermod was there and had uncorked a bottle of
wine – and after gasping with delight I drank their health. And then
we talked of other things – with pauses which were filled with joy –

Then Rachel ran upstairs to tell Molly who was unwell and in bed –
and I after her. Molly was reading, I suppose for the tenth time, Pride
and Prejudice – She had just finished Mr Darcy's proposal! Her face
suddenly became young with delight as I saw again that brilliant
museful sparkle on it I loved so much.

Arlington Street and Hatfield

J. H. TUNNELL

*Mr Tunnell first went to Arlington Street as the telephone
footman for two weeks in 1935. He finally retired having
been butler to three marquesses in 1977. His wife
worked in the stillroom at Hatfield and Arlington Street.
He has written down some of his recollections.*

LORD David was sent to the village Post Office with a telegram from
his mother, (Alice 4th Marchioness). The Postmaster was unable
to read it and sent Lord David back to his mother for clarification.
Unfortunately she too was unable to read it.

I remember Lord David in Arlington Street about to attend a family
wedding in St Margaret's, Westminster. He got in to the waiting taxi
and the driver closed the door and got back into his seat. During these
few seconds Lord David realised that he had no buttonhole so hopped
out of the taxi, using the other side, to cross over to the flower selling
lady who stood on the corner outside the 'Blue Post' pub to purchase a
buttonhole. The taxi driver drove off, unaware that he had no fare.
What happened when he arrived at St Margaret's, I never heard.

Another time I remember Lord David coming to Hatfield for the
weekend. I could not find any socks in his suitcase and he was due to go
to London on the Monday morning. I informed him of the situation
and he replied 'Oh, that's alright, I'll just wear my spats.'

Lord Salisbury said to me that whenever Lord David wanted money,
I was to give it to him. One day he asked me if I could 'Lend him ten
shillings', so I started counting it out then he said: 'Well a pound would
be *very* nice.'

Lord and Lady David came to stay with his parents at Cranborne
Lodge after their son Jonathan was born. On seeing Lord David I
congratulated him. He thanked me and said 'Isn't it wonderful what
one can do!'

MRS TUNNELL *adds:* Lord David arrived at Cranborne Lodge minus his overcoat. Lady David said 'Where is your overcoat, darling?' He said he did not know. 'Oh David it is the third one you have lost this year.'

Lady Salisbury (4th Marchioness) invited us up for Christmas but we could not go so instead we went up on Boxing Day. I sat beside Lord David and I remember we talked about the painting of him with his mother. by J J Shannon painted in 1908. I said to him 'you were a very pretty little boy. my Lord!' 'Oh no!' he said 'I was a very pale child'. He smiled and said 'The artist made me look pretty – but I do remember being very proud of the velvet suit I wore.'

The Young Don

ELIZABETH LONGFORD

*Lady Longford is the wife of Frank Pakenham, 7th Earl of
Longford. Biographer of Queen Elizabeth, the Queen Mother,
she has written many books including* Victoria RI, Wellington,
Years of the Sword *(1969) and* Pillar of State *(1972).
She went up to Oxford in 1926 where she
met and became friends with David.*

I OWE David Cecil more moments of delight at Oxford than anyone
else though I read classics there and therefore did not attend his
lectures or tutorials.

He was the best of all conversationalists; our common friend
Maurice Bowra then Dean of Wadham being the best of all talkers.
The difference was clear cut. While Maurice would build up laughter
single-handed, his jokes created of entirely personal idiosyncracies,
flashing wit, rollicking paradoxes and puns, David would draw out
everyone round the table, making them feel that they were one and all
in superlative form. David orchestrated the jokes, Maurice was a
soloist.

David nearly always discussed people rather than ideas: what made
them tick – or fail to get themselves properly wound up.

One often assumes that a pinch of malice is essential for this. David's
brilliance, however, was without hurtfulness. Perhaps for this reason I
never heard a really malicious story against him. In fact it would be
truer to say that all the stories which might contain a critical innuendo
were told by David against himself.

There was the memory of his capering around Tom Quad as an
undergraduate, chanting, 'I am drunk as the lord that I am!' There was
the joke about the Berlin night-club in Christopher Isherwood days when
a German homosexual came up to him and enquired *'Sind Sie Normal?'*
To which David, who had a touch of hypochondria when young,

replied, 'Funny you should ask. As a matter of fact I *did* have a slight temperature when I started out.' His extreme pallor and slight figure made him look delicate as well as poetic, possibly taking in himself as well as some of his friends. Yet it only needed Rachel's wonderful combination of care and commonsense to set him on the long, happy road towards a vigorous old age.

Another story concerns David's first visit to one of the Eastern States of the USA. I remember how vividly he described a conversation between his all-too generous hosts and himself, the shy young Englishman.

'Lord David, you're English so of course you love fox-hunting?'

David, though he regarded hunting in Oscar Wilde's phrase as the unspeakable in pursuit of the uneatable, nevertheless thought it unnecessary to disappoint his kind hosts by saying so. After all, the Atlantic now rolled between him and the hunting shires. There seemed no danger of having his prowess put to the test. To his horror his hosts told him that they had anticipated his wishes and a hunt had been laid on for tomorrow. When tomorrow dawned there was no English lord to be seen. David had discovered that he had some urgent proofs to correct. Of course there were no proofs, so David spent the empty day playing the pianola. When the hunting party returned unexpectedly early, David panicked, tore out the giveaway music roll and threw it behind the pianola – where it was clearly visible to his surprised hosts.

Soon after Frank and I were married (in 1931) David invited us to stay with his parents at Hatfield. He did not explain that when I went up to change for dinner, the floor in front of the blazing fire in our bedroom would have opened up, to reveal a sunken bath tub level with the carpet and ready to be filled with hot water from lovely copper cans. What David *did* explain was that next morning there would be family prayers in the chapel – women on one side, men on the other. I was impressed by the complete naturalness with which he introduced the subject; one that even in those days was not a usual part of countryhouse life. But to David there was no need to explain away or apologise for religion: it was just as real an aspect of existence as work or games.

This attitude must have been largely due to David's father, the Marquess of Salisbury. *Jem* Salisbury – I can still hear his friend and contemporary, Ettie Desborough, lingering over Lord Salisbury's name with loving relish – *Jem* was at once a saint and a reactionary. From him David learned to imbibe genuine goodness, while realising that goodness could be dissociated from political beliefs. When he came to write his famous two-part biography of Lord Melbourne, *The Young Melbourne* and '*Lord M*', he was able to demonstrate the separateness of religion and politics, but in reverse. Viscount Melbourne, unlike the Marquess of Salisbury, was no saint, but neither were his political views negligible. Though David's father was an uncompromising Tory, his mother came from the Whig family of Gore. David himself was soon analysing the great Whig houses of the eighteenth and nineteenth centuries with as much empathy as he was later to apply to the House of Cecil. If anything, he gave 'Lord M' too great a benefit of the doubt, especially in his dealings with the young infatuated Victoria. What if Prince Albert had not arrived on the scene when he did? Might not Melbourne's cynicism and moral ineptitude (*vide* his handling of the disgraceful Lady Flora Hastings affair) have come near to corrupting the impressionable Queen?

Such speculation is thoroughly donnish. But for that reason David would have enjoyed it. For he was in a sense the ideal young don: always ready to give help, to stimulate argument, to set up amusing subjects for discussion. I remember when he came to stay at Pakenham Hall (now restored to its original name of Tullynally) before any of us except Edward and Christine Longford were married. David started off some scholarly and imaginative table-talk on the subject of *War and Peace*, claiming that Frank was the image of Pierre in that novel. I was ashamed to confess that I had not yet read that great work of genius and so was in no position to challenge or welcome David's thesis – as I might have done ten years later, when the phoney war was to set us poring over masterpieces of literature in the blackout.

David visited Pakenham in August 1931. While there, he spent a day or so in bed with the usual 'slight temperature'. He had played in the Cavan tennis tournament as Frank's partner, for despite his apparent frailty he was an effective player. A sick member of a house-party is not generally the most popular of guests; but such was the charm of David's conversation that there was always a large attentive audience around his bed. He was well up to contributing to the joys of our last evening when he sang in plaintive tones:

> My mother's an apple-pie maker,
> My father he fiddles for gin,
> My sister walks streets for her living –
> Good God! How the money rolls in!

Like all the Cecils and their clan, David was a master of after-dinner games. It was he who introduced us to that entertaining exercise in psychological ingenuity, 'What flows in so-and-so's veins?' The liquid could vary from sap to Jeyes Fluid.

To have David staying at Pakenham was only equalled by staying with him in Venice. There were four of us in L P Hartley's palazzo that April 1931: Leslie himself, David's close friend; Mary Pakenham (later Clive) my future sister-in-law; David and me. Rachel should have been there also, for David and she were in love. I realised this while travelling out with David by wagon-lit. At one point he drew from his pocket a long, closely written letter. It was from Rachel: being her beautifully expressed feelings about April in England, with due regard to the fact that David, like Robert Browning, was in Italy. We agreed that Rachel had the perceptions of a poet. I could see that this was one of the things that the young English don wanted in his beloved. When I got to know Rachel later on I found that her feeling for Wordsworthian poetry was balanced by a strong, dramatic sense of comedy. One of the funniest performances was a skit on her school elocution teacher's rendering of *Drake's Drum*. The sweep of Rachel's arm and the pseudo-professional crescendo of her voice as she 'turned and finished the game' were inimitable: quite as good as David's imitation of a gushing lady asking Margot Asquith, mother of the future film director, Puffin Asquith, 'And how is your little Penguin?'

David was also a connoisseur of political anecdotes, two of which Frank remembers. A young MP ran into Mr Baldwin the Prime Minister in the lobby and said to him: 'I should like to talk to you about co-partnership.' Baldwin, resting his hand on the MP's shoulder, replied: 'My dear boy, I could talk to you about it for hours.' Next moment he had vanished.

At the time of Appeasement in 1938, 'Bobbety' Cranborne, (later Salisbury) David's brother, was under-secretary at the Foreign Office. He resigned, along with Eden the Foreign Secretary, from the Government of Neville Chamberlain. 'Bobbety's' uncle Lord Robert Cecil – the Cecils held no brief for the Chamberlains, incidentally my family! – sent a message: 'A bas les bourgeois'.

Helpful kindness was normally an outstanding feature of David's character. With him it was both an instinct and a moral imperative. My husband, Frank Pakenham (later Longford) returned as a don to Oxford in 1940, after a rather inglorious eight months in the war-time army. David cheered him up with a display of affection that seemed to spring from a deep spiritual source, and at the same time involved no effort but was perfectly natural and spontaneous. No one was so good at morale-boosting as David, because of this gift. This emphatically did not mean that he felt it a duty to be nice to people. His religion was so much part of him – his nature and upbringing – that it never occurred to him to behave in any other way.

Whether it was depressed colleagues or girl students, his magic worked with them all. Our third daughter was Rachel's goddaughter and called after her. 'Have you any special memories of David at Oxford?' I asked her. 'Sunday mornings at 12 o'clock. On alternate Sundays David would hand out huge goblets of sherry. Of course being Sunday none of us had had any breakfast. Just tumbled out of bed. We rolled home feeling much better.'

I myself was tremendously helped by David when I was writing a biography of Queen Elizabeth the Queen Mother whom he knew well. The point is not that he helped me – I would have taken that for granted – but that, like the true scholar he was, he took the trouble to draft his random thoughts into written words, resulting in a stylish, original and lucid contribution to my book – and to the understanding of his much loved friend.

In the last analysis it was the mingling of wit and sympathy that made David's company so uniquely attractive. I have a letter I wrote to my mother from Oxford in my third year: 'Last night I dined with David Cecil, who was so funny that I laughed the complexion off my face.' When he won the Hawthornden Prize for *The Stricken Deer*, his biography of the poet Cowper who went melancholy mad, the other side of his nature had come into play and was being acclaimed. His friends felt it was the right prize for the right person on the right subject.

Churchill has told us that Lenin's sympathies were 'cold and wide as the Arctic Ocean, his hatreds tight as the hangman's noose.' David had no hatreds. And his sympathies were warm and deep as his friends' needs, whether the friends were within the covers of his books or in the many strata of Oxford life.

When I First Met David

MARY CLIVE

*Lady Mary Clive is a sister of Lord Longford. She was in
her early twenties when she and David became friends.*

As soon as I met David I took a fancy to him. Although he was an
Oxford don and had written a life of Cowper which had won
several prizes he was engagingly boyish and very friendly. He was pale
and interesting and poetic-looking. Even his clothes were somehow
picturesque. Compared to most modern young men he seemed almost
a fairy prince. Naturally I hoped to meet him again and I was delighted
when, at the end of 1930, my brother Frank arranged that he and I and
David and Frank's semi-fiancée Elizabeth should all go together to
spend a few days with my brother Edward and his wife Christine, who
had a castle in Ireland.

Our only fellow-guest turned out to be an extraordinary young man
called John Betjeman. Of course nobody then guessed that one day he
would be world-famous but already he had the knack of making
people join in his games; soon we had all succumbed to Betjemania and
were capering about singing revivalist hymns. Perhaps this was not
exactly David's idea of fun but he was swept in with the rest and
anyway the non-stop chatter was very amusing. I remember that one
night at dinner someone said that there could be a Shakespearean
sonnet about banking, beginning, 'Now my account is closed, my
passbook full,' and the party produced thirteen more lines which
rhymed and scanned and sounded just like Shakespeare.

We left on New Year's Eve and shared a four-berth sleeper and felt
enormously dashing – we were none of us very sophisticated – and at
midnight we joined hands and sang Auld Lang Syne. I was in a top
bunk and as I was dropping off to sleep two objects whizzed past my
head and into the rack; they were David's spats which he wore to keep
his feet warm.

Our Irish trip had been such a success that in April David invited Elizabeth and me to stay in Venice with his friend Leslie Hartley. Leslie lived in bachelor comfort in a furnished flat which looked out onto a side canal and was just what a literary man's hideout ought to be. We all got on fine. Leslie was cosy and liked the company of females as much as David did, and although he was older than David and they came from very different backgrounds, they suited each other very well and in fact remained lifelong friends. Besides being a novelist, Leslie wrote reviews, so the latest books were lying about his sitting-room, and I remember how we laughed over Linklater's *Juan in America* and also that David introduced me to the works of Hemingway. Thrown in with the flat was a sumptuous gondola adorned with gilded carvings and turkey carpets not to mention a handsome gondolier, and we spent afternoons floating about the lagoon while David read Keats aloud. Written down, this all sounds rather tame but the week shines in my memory as one of the most blissful in my life. At the end of it David hired a car (and driver) and conducted Elizabeth and me round Padua and Ravenna and Bologna. At Bologna he was smitten by some sort of chill and we found him dosing himself with whisky in the hotel bar, looking deathlike against a background of super-modern jazz decor; however, he assured us that he was often taken in this way and that he could manage perfectly well, so we went off to Rome and left him to his fate.

It may be that David's fragile health accounted for many of his peculiarities. He had been a delicate child and had been more at home than most little boys. I imagine that, being very much the youngest of the family and an amusing and precocious child, he became a sort of mascot in a house full of clever and distinguished grown-ups. At Eton he still was considered delicate and was let off games, but he seems to have got through his time there not unpleasantly.

In *Oliver Twist* there is an old man who divides boys into mealy boys and beef-faced boys and it was perfectly clear to which class David belonged. He had no wish whatever to be a beef-faced boy and he avoided hearties as much as possible but he was always haunted by a slight fear that some day he would be cornered.

I was once on a Greek cruise with David and as we chugged peacefully among the islands he suddenly asked, 'What shall we do if the crew mutinies?' He need not have worried. He was never tested by a crisis of that sort, and as a matter of fact when the Cruise coaches raced each other and most of the passengers were frightened and furious, David enjoyed the excitement and afterwards took the trouble to go and congratulate the driver.

I used to have a craze for asking people what they would choose if they were allowed to tell one lie to St Peter. 'I would say that I was immensely brave,' said David immediately. When I repeated this to Leslie Hartley he remarked 'It would be more to the point if David said that he had never chucked a dinner engagement.'

It was generally known that a girl called Rachel MacCarthy was in love with David and eventually in June 1931 we met, when Elizabeth (now officially engaged to Frank), and I went down to Oxford for a Commem ball. We were staying at the Randolph Hotel and so was Rachel, and in somewhat critical mood we marched along the corridor to her room. The door was opened by a little person out of a Kate Greenaway picture with a smiling face and bright alert eyes that missed nothing, and I decided on the spot that since she loved David, he had better marry her.

It was easy to turn acquaintance into friendship because Rachel lived in Wellington Square and I lodged just the other side of the King's Road. The first time that I called at her house I was shown into a room where her father was telephoning; he was *en deshabille* with his face covered in lather, but such was his social adroitness that not only was he unembarrassed himself but he did not make me feel embarrassed either. Desmond MacCarthy was a distinguished literary journalist who moved easily between Mayfair, Bloomsbury and Bohemia so Rachel had seen many kinds of cultivated coterie. She also had two brothers and plenty of cousins but the way of life which had really captured her imagination is that depicted in the novels of Henry James. She was a very funny mimic and had trained at RADA and on qualifying was offered the part of Nina in Tyrone Guthrie's production of the Seagull at his new Festival Theatre, Cambridge. However, she had just met David, and although she was so humble about herself that she did not expect he would ever marry her, she felt she could not bear to become part of the theatrical world, and she abandoned her career and instead did some rather nebulous secretarial jobs. Her parents, though chronically hard up, do not seem to have raised any objections.

One beautiful autumn day I went with David to lunch at Hatfield and was entranced by the whole set-up. Considering the grandeur of the house, the atmosphere was noticeably relaxed. Dotted around the rooms were some of the relations about whom David had so often reminisced – clever, amusing idiosyncratic, high-minded, worldly people. In the Armoury children were riding tricycles.

The matriarch of the tribe was Lady Salisbury, David's mother, a stout Edwardian lady with a loud, jolly laugh; generous and benevolent, she took a passionate interest in everybody though somewhat hampered by the constrictions imposed by her position – her grandchildren were amazed to discover that she had never had a meal in a London restaurant. She was the great-grand-daughter of Lord Melbourne's sister and she possessed cardboard boxes full of old letters. Through her, David felt that the Regency beau-monde was all part of the family. Lord Salisbury, on the other hand, was mild and remote with the unexpected gift of being able to describe events so graphically that one almost felt that one had been an eye-witness.

David always said that his favourite home was Cranborne and he certainly preferred literature to politics, but he was very much one of the Cecils of Hatfield.

David had now given up Oxford with the intention of being a full-time writer and he was established, as if by magic, in a house in Edwardes Square which, like all his subsequent houses, was pretty and welcoming and Jane Austenish. In November I set off to go round the world and as a farewell present he gave me (besides some scent) pocket editions of *Emma*, *Rob Roy* and Boswell's *Journal of a Tour to the Hebrides* – ideal companions for long and boring sea voyages.

In the following June I returned to London and there was David again, as nice as ever. Gossip said that he was planning to get married but that he could not make up his mind which girl to select, the trouble apparently being that he wanted to fall passionately in love like Anna Karenina and the people in *Wuthering Heights* and he did not seem able to accomplish this feat although he was taking out at least four girls – in those days it was quite usual to dine with a different person every night of the week. David was attracted by the idea of elegant vampires and flattered himself that he knew how to get on with them, but was actually appealed to by girls who aroused his protective instincts. Once, years later, talking about Chopin and his affair with George Sand, he remarked that that sort of man was usually drawn towards masterful women but in his own case it was the reverse – he liked to be made to feel strong and masculine.

At last David got into such a state of agitation that he went abroad to consult the family shrink, who evidently gave him some very good advice, for when he came home he rushed round to Wellington Square and (according to his own account) fell on his knees in front of Rachel and said 'Will you marry me?' She gave one look of horrified surprise and replied, 'Yes, and I've always wanted to.'

So in the autumn there was a grand Cecil wedding and they both lived happily ever afterwards.

Looking at David's life as a whole what strikes me is that, though he was constantly in a flap and a dither about little things, when it came to important matters he showed the utmost good sense. He was on the best of terms with all generations of his enormous family, he chose a profession which was congenial to him, and he wrote the books he wanted to write. He knew his own limits and he kept within them. He might drop crumbs on the floor but he was not unlucky or accident prone and, as far as I can remember, if one made an arrangement with him, it went perfectly smoothly.

David as Seen by a Young Girl

Vivien White is a daughter of Augustus
and Dorelia John.

DAVID often came over to Fryern Court from Rockbourne with his charming wife Rachel. They were a very special couple and Augustus, not surprisingly, painted them both which made their visits more frequent.

At the tea table, the talk would become magical, and I basked and blossomed in it. David was one of those who brought people out. This took a bit of doing in my case, and I blush now to think of how I must have aired my views on writers, many of whom David knew personally. But nothing seemed to offend him and there was always an enthusiastic response to my floundering enquiries. His beautiful looks, his long sensitive hands with their gesticulations captured my heart. Rachel seemed quite undisturbed by my obvious adoration of her husband and was always very kind to me.

They often came to our evening parties and to picnics on the Wiltshire Downs. The evening parties usually ended with pulling the carpet back and dancing. Many an ecstatic waltz did I dance with David, as luckily he also seemed to love the Viennese Waltzes, which we played on our wonderful E.M.G. wind-up gramophone. We must have cut an unusual figure whirling round and round on the dining room floor. I suppose the summers at Fryern and our way of life must have appealed to the Cecils; at least I hope so. They were not afflicted by the darker side of the John entourage.

We were all so happy when they came over. One evening though the Cecils had to leave early before any dancing or exciting talk could take place. I retired to my bedroom and lay on my bed in floods of tears; then I became aware that Dorelia was standing in the doorway, and,

[63]

wringing her hands, she entreated me not to take things so seriously but to return downstairs and join in.

I was very surprised because we so seldom involved one another in our personal ups and downs. I recall pulling myself together sufficiently to go back to the party and of course nobody had noticed my absence.

PART THREE

1940 – 1949

1940 – 1949

DURING the war Rachel spent part of her time with Jonathan at Rockbourne where David would join them at weekends. E. Q. Nicholson, a childhood friend of Rachel's and daughter-in-law of the artist William Nicholson recalls being evacuated there. 'In 1940 a bomb fell in the garden of our house in Fareham. Because of the obvious danger I had already moved my three children to my mother's house in Marlow. I returned from Fareham, knowing that it was quite impossible to remain with my mother for more than a few days. I telephoned Rachel and the following day my three children all under five, two nannies, a pekinese and myself all moved in on the Cecil household where we remained for six months. It was before the very severe petrol rationing and David used to come and go between Oxford and Rockbourne, Rachel sometimes with him and sometimes remaining at Rockbourne. I remember how very happy they were.'

The following story illustrates how very unsuited David was to war-time emergencies of any kind. They often stayed with David's sister Mima Harlech at Brogyntyn. One time, soon after they arrived, there was an immense explosion and a German pilot leading a raid on Liverpool dropped a bomb in a field, killing two cows and shattering some of the windows in the house. David immediately switched on a light to see what was happening.

David's great friend Isaiah Berlin went to the United States in 1941 where he was a British Propagandist 'seeking to drag America into the war.' He wrote a letter to the Ministry of Information and to the Foreign Office suggesting that David should go to Washington in some capacity, but his letter was ignored. Isaiah Berlin says 'because I thought he would be very useful; this highly intelligent friend of mine would charm the Americans, and I thought it would be so nice for me. When I asked David whether he had ever been approached, he said: "never".'

David and Rachel's second son Hugh was born in 1943. The house in Rockbourne was let to Leslie Hartley where he started writing *The Eustace and Hilda Trilogy*. They returned during the holidays, but were now living in a flat in Savile House. David continued to teach at New College as well as write. He published *Hardy, the Novelist* in 1943, *Two Quiet Lives* in 1948 and *Poets and Storytellers* in 1949.

Isaiah Berlin observed a gradual shift in David's moralism. 'When, in the thirties and he was at Wadham, he was a pious properly communicant member of the Church of England. He strongly disapproved of divorce and of adultery. He really was against it. When Sir Thomas Beecham's name came up as a possible Honorary Fellow of Wadham, David voted against it on the grounds that he was a philanderer. So he had to wait till David resigned from Wadham before he was elected. Much later, there was a question of whether to make my colleague Stuart Hampshire a Fellow of New College. He was 'living in sin.' David was in torture. He didn't want to vote with the reactionaries, he wanted to vote with us. At the meeting he couldn't make up his mind. First of all David lifted his hand to vote against, then lowered it again, and in the end he didn't vote. David liked him particularly and thought him both charming and sensitive. In the end I remember going to dine with Lady Cunard who was a fairly notorious lady. David said 'I hear you are dining with Emerald Cunard. Do you think you might suggest that I come to dinner too? She'll probably think I'm a frightful prude – I'm not you know. I really like people like that.' And she did. There was a shift and I have seen both phases but all that melted away and he adapted.'

After the war David was offered a job at Cambridge as Professor of English. This was a great step forward for a don and he agonized over it. He had narrowly missed an Oxford professorship and it seemed unlikely that another opportunity would present itself. He decided against it: the upheaval would have been tremendous, his children were at school in Oxford, all his friends and past life were there. That year, 1947, their daughter Laura was born.

Jonathan Cecil writes:

'Oxford friends from the war and post-war years included the novelist Joyce Cary with whom my father had some of his most passionate discussions about art and life, the flamboyant Enid Starkie, ever generous with her meat ration, Roy and Billa Harrod, sophisticated party givers, the sometimes cantankerous Dame Helen Gardiner and the benignly booming Hugo Dyson. Among pupils were Rachel

Trickett, John Bayley, Frank Hauser and John Bamborough. Especial delights were 'church-crawling' in John Betjeman's battered car and visits to his house at Wantage: the wonderfully eccentric Roman Catholic convert Penelope Betjeman once terminated a telephone conversation with my father by squawking "Well I must go – I'm talking to the governess about the Precious Blood."'

'He was a marvellous tutor, of that there is no doubt' Sir Isaiah Berlin recalls: 'All those pupils at New College who became dons were very very grateful to him.' And he continues 'he was the best company there has ever been, I miss him more than anybody. He was wittier and more amusing about other people. Little vignettes. He had a very sharp eye for personal and social idiosyncracies. David could get on with anybody if he chose to.'

In 1949 David did become a professor. He was made the first Goldsmith's Professor of English Literature at Oxford. His inaugural lecture in May was 'The Fine Art of Reading,' published in 1957.

David's dislike of the Germans was still in evidence after the war. Appearing on the Brain's Trust, he referred to Goethe as "that great German gasbag" which shocked Julian Huxley. For some reason this prejudice did not prevent them hiring German nannies, one of whom turned out to be a morbid but unrepentant Nazi called Ursula. Laura remembers her own amazement as Ursula was the first adult whom she saw crying. Then there was a crazed nanny called Paula. Her parents were dead, they had been bombed and everything destroyed. Before the war there had been another German who turned out to be a spy. She was sent to Rockbourne and was supposed to keep her ears open. Years later she telephoned. She was no longer a spy, but rich and comfortable.

HC

A Colleague's Wife

BILLA HARROD

*Lady Harrod is the widow of the distinguished
economist Roy Harrod, who for many years was a close
Oxford colleague and friend.*

D AVID was one of my husband Roy's best friends and he was one of
the first people I met when we married. They were still living in
Rockbourne then, but, when David came back to Oxford as a don,
they lived in a flat in the High Street, the first of the three Oxford
homes they had.

Jonathan and Henry are almost exactly the same age, and I well
remember nursery teas in the High Street with the two babies and their
nannies; I remember bringing little bottles of swede juice because there
were no oranges in those early war years.

David and Roy were very sympathetic and affectionate fathers,
though of course not practical like fathers are now: I remember seeing
David trying to switch off a fuming electric kettle in Rachel's room
when she was in bed after one of her babies. He darted about the room
struggling wildly to find the right place, while the room filled with
steam. He was so kind and so devoted and I find it difficult to think of
him apart from Rachel. Unfortunately I didn't see him after Rachel
died. His conversation is what I most remember, fascinating words
poured out very fast in his rather high voice. He could *never* be dull.

Driving with him was exciting because he would take both hands off
the wheel and turn right round to tell you something. Rachel described
this rather well in *Theresa's Choice*, but she transfers it to riding a
horse.

He had perfect taste in everything, except food, which neither he nor
Rachel cared for, but Solly Zuckerman had a story about David
producing a very excellent bottle of champagne, in the war, when such
things were scarce, and telling Solly that he had got it from the college

cellars for 7/- – which seemed natural to him but to Solly a miracle.

He had wonderful, natural good manners, rather rare in Oxford, and was always delightfully welcoming and easy to talk to about any subject, including local gossip, though he was never unkind – again an untraditional Oxford approach. Although a very serious and dutiful Oxford don, he always seemed like a breath of the wider and more interesting world, though he was utterly unsnobbish and not remotely a name-dropper; there was no need for that in David's personality.

He was Dominick's godfather and I am Laura's godmother; we stayed with each other in the country and were all often together as families through nursery, Dragon School and Eton life. He and Rachel were among the best of our Oxford friends; Oxford without them, and a few others like Frank and Elizabeth Pakenham, would have been a bit grim and dull, especially in the war years.

David was very encouraging and appreciative of other people's efforts; he must have been a wonderful tutor, and his lectures were superb. People who had no right to attend them used to borrow gowns so as to look like undergraduates and get in. He spoke with great enthusiasm and was a real inspiration and opened many eyes to unexpected pleasures in books. I had always thought *Lark Rise to Candleford* sounded rather twee, but he told me how good Flora Thomson was, for which I am deeply grateful.

Of course his real knowledge and erudition went far beyond Flora Thomson, but it was typical that she was included in his favourites, as indeed was Barbara Pym.

David's Closest Friend

L. P. HARTLEY

*The novelist Leslie Hartley wrote this introduction
to David's "Festschrift" which was a volume of essays and
poems presented to David on his retirement from
Oxford, edited by Wallace Robson, published in 1970.*

I FIRST met Lord David Cecil at Oxford in the Hilary Term of 1919. I
had been invalided out of the Army a year before. He had just come
up from Eton, so there was a considerable gap between our ages.

Like seeks like, and by a sort of bush-telegraph sometimes finds it;
and so it was that one evening, walking down the High, I met David
Cecil. Probably we had met before, but, although I did not know him,
or he me, we recognized in each other what I like to think was a
kindred spirit and a friendship began which has lasted through the
years.

I often think of my friends as being of the same age as when I first
met them, and of myself as being much the same age too. How absurd
it seems, and in my case is, the image of youth stamped on age! But it
isn't absurd in the case of David Cecil, who still has the air of youth
and the manner of the youth that he then was. There were many others
who had just come to Oxford as ardent as he was. There were his
relations and friends on whom the war had left its mark of horror and
sadness, but not the indelible bruise of actual experience from which
(for instance) Siegfried Sassoon, Osbert Sitwell, and Edmund Blunden
suffered.

The new-comers – Eddy Sackville-West, Anthony Asquith, and how
many others – only knew the war as a disappearing shadow. They
helped to form a circle into which I, though much their senior, found a
place. We met constantly in each others' rooms and outside, at
Garsington Manor, the hospitable home of Lady Ottoline Morrell,
and at The Wharf, where Lord and Lady Oxford, in their different

[72]

ways, taught the young idea how to shoot. These extra-mural centres of culture, though less academically formidable than a session with one's tutor, were critical as well as encouraging, and demanded that one put one's best foot forward.

Of course ours was a very small circle among a multitude of circles, a few of them concentric, but mostly not, but it would not be too much to say that for ours David Cecil held a torch – not for war heroes, or anti-war heroes, but for people who led quiet lives, studious and sociable, into which the idea of violence never entered – people temperamentally akin to the subjects of some of the books he was later to write – Dorothy Osborne, William Cowper, Thomas Gray, Jane Austen, and last but not least Max Beerbohm – unsensational figures but none the less servants of literature, whose contribution to art maintained a steady level and even an upward trend, preserving what can be preserved, and increasing what can be increased, without the help of major convulsions or violence of any sort, within the special public for whom they wrote, or outside.

But although David Cecil's *penchant*, as a biographer, has been for quiet lives, as a critic, especially as a critic of fiction, his sympathies range more widely. This does not imply any diminution in the strength of his opinions, for or against, or the vigour with which he expressed them. An old friend of mine had a book-plate inscribed, 'Passionately prejudiced, passionately attached', and this could be said of David Cecil, who has seldom been in doubt of his feelings or his judgement (which depends in some measure on his feelings) where a work of literature is concerned. For example, his unswerving admiration for Sir Walter Scott, Jane Austen, Emily Brontë and Thomas Hardy – a sufficiently wide range of sympathy. And in these latter days when 'the wear and tear of discrimination' as Henry James called it, has increased with the increase of published books, he has never hesitated to utter, regardless of fashion, and without fear or favour, opinions expected or unexpected, but always his own.

A book-reviewer for about twenty years, with sometimes six or seven books a week to read and write about, I have rather lost my taste for what Lord David has called 'the fine art of reading'; but he has not. In his time he has probably read more books than most people, certainly more than I have; but in my case it was compulsory; in his case it was and still is compulsive. He is an omnivorous reader and if left alone for five minutes in a room with books he will take out half a dozen, scatter them over floor, chairs and tables and almost literally devour them — for they sometimes fall apart between his fingers, so eager is he to get at their contents.

He is not only the quickest reader I have ever known but also the quickest to extract the pith and marrow of the book; a sixth sense leads him at once to his aim, even if at the same time he is engaged in conversation — this way and that dividing his swift mind.

One reason why his work has a perennial freshness is that the idea, the inspiration, has come to him in a flash, and the flash continues to illuminate it, whatever labour the task of research and exposition has cost him. For quick as his mind is to seize on a point, he is prepared to face much drudgery to prove and exemplify it. To my mind one of his finest achievements in the field of literary ctiticism is his theory of Emily Brontë's basic intention in *Wuthering Heights*. By the house and household of Wuthering Heights — whether presided over by the drunkard Hindley or filched from him by the villian Heathcliff — she means to represent the storm, the aberration from normal human nature. Whereas Thrushcross Grange, in spite of its many vicissitudes, embodies the calm, the restoration of order out of chaos, which wins in the end, after and indeed before Heathcliff's death.

This theory is paralleled in Emily Brontë's poems by her insistence on the dichotomy between North and South, between Gondal with its ice and snow and Gaaldine with 'its tropic flowers and rivers running free'. Emily's sympathies may have been with the storm rather than the calm, and I think they were; but it was left to David Cecil to discern the broad fundamental contrast between the two worlds of *Wuthering Heights*.

This is only one instance of his vital contributions to literary criticism, and only one instance of his power, through imaginative insight into his subject, to make the sometimes dry bones of literary criticism live. By means of apt quotation and illustration he is able to season the analytical with the objective, so that we can almost see as well as read his thoughts. Someone said disparagingly of a certain writer, 'with him all words are free and equal'. This could never be said of David Cecil, to whom words are mint-fresh, new coins bearing the impress of his personality and his personal vision.

What is the secret of his critical gift that distinguishes it from others? Partly, I think, his individual approach, which is easy to recognize but hard to define, because it combines the qualities of the professional and the amateur. Professional in its seriousness, its technical proficiency and its regard for the subject; amateur (in the original sense) of loving or liking the subject too much to let himself be bound by hard-and-fast rules of treatment. The discipline of professionalism is relaxed every now and then by intrusions of the amateur, as it was with Coleridge, who would fly off at a tangent when a thought struck him that was only on the periphery of his subject but which related it to kindred thoughts that were present in his mind.

And so with David Cecil; his love of literature is too strong a thing to be forced into the channel of a single theme. It overflows its banks for the mere pleasure of it – and as all his readers know, to give pleasure is one of his main objects in writing. Writing without pleasure, given and received, is dead: it is one of the essential differences between art and science. All work and no play makes Jack a dull boy, and it is the 'playward' (as Thomas Hardy' might have said) element in David Cecil's writing, its darting, ranging qualities, finding analogies in the other arts, that saves it from ever being a treadmill or a tram-line.

These are some of the attributes of his mind and they are reflected in his appearance, slightly dandified, with a tie or a waistcoat that one doesn't quite expect; his hair which seems to move as rapidly and take on as many aspects as his mind, and his gestures, which are so much his own, fidgety but not irritable. His feet, rocking to and fro from his knees, might be thought to be kicking an imaginary football; the sudden outflung movement of his arms and hands, might be dismissive of something he has just said, or a spontaneous recognition of a truth that someone else has just said. His whole being, physical and mental, seems to act together, and represent the same thing. There is no one I know who is more of a piece than David Cecil, no one who is more himself, be the circumstances what they may.

Of this his pupils at Oxford and the undergraduates who attended his lectures must be well aware, and of the gift he has for addressing the whole of himself to his subject and his audience. The sudden smile, amused or self-deprecatory, the flick of the slender hand with its incredibly long fingers – the whole armoury of vocal and physical persuasion which turns a lecture into something like a dramatic performance – how did he develop this technique of putting himself *en rapport* with his listeners?

Few of his contemporary undergraduates would have guessed that this frail slight figure, with its loping, plunging gait, almost a sprite, a leprechaun, was not just an apparition sent to be a moment's ornament, but had in him the stamina to become one of the University's best-known and best-loved teachers.

He did not achieve this position easily. No one who has heard him speak, either on the platform or anywhere else, and warmed to the excitement that boils up so quickly in him, can imagine, if they have not actually witnessed it, the almost agony that the written word causes him. Surely no writer, not even Flaubert, can have suffered more from the toil, and from being in the toils, of literary composition.

We were staying in Venice when he was writing part of *The Stricken Deer* and I shall never forget the tortured features, the despairing gestures, the body thrown this way and that, which accompanied the writing of a sentence which afterwards read as if it had rolled off his pen.

It was only then I realized how much his brilliance as a talker was balanced by his hardships as a writer. His impulse to communicate, to give out by word of mouth to his friends, was almost inhibited by the conscientiousness that afflicted him when he had to put pen to paper. Then, the obligation of the biographer to factual truth and the obligation of the artist to the language it should be put in – for each weighs equally with David Cecil – might well have ended in a stalemate, a blank page. And I often thought that if my standard was as high as his, and if it cost me as much mental energy with its accompanying frustration as it cost him, I should have ceased from mental fight and let my pen sleep in my hand.

He did not have to write, he did not have to rely on writing or teaching for his living, but he chose the hard way, partly because his impulse to write was stronger than his impulse to resist writing, and also because the 'noblesse oblige' feeling of his family, diverted in his case from politics to literature, forbade him to bury the talent that he knew he had and that *au fond* he enjoyed using, whatever pains it cost him.

We have, I suppose, an obligation towards the memory of the illustrious dead, and few have done more to fulfil this obligation, or fulfilled it with a better will and a better grace than David Cecil has. He has never tried to whitewash a black character, or blacken a white one. No racist he.

Neither biography nor criticism can strictly be called creative writings any more than history can be; the imaginative element in such works has to be severely disciplined. But in a slightly different sense criticism and biography can be creative; they can create a new way of looking at and treating a subject, as Dr Johnson did, as Coleridge did, as Lytton Strachey did, as T. S. Eliot did, as Edmund Wilson did – to quote only a few names of those whose contribution to literature has been primarily through the mind aided by the imagination, not vice versa. And the presence of the author in his work, if felt strongly enough, as in the case of David Cecil, also serves as a kind of creativity, for without it the dish would lack the flavour and the savour which (to use a homely metaphor) the cook has put in. The ingredients may not be his own; but his presentation of them can fairly be called creative, more so than would be the case with some writers who rely solely on their imaginations. Style itself is a creation; and no one who reads a page of David Cecil's work could doubt that it was by him, and no other.

Here are two personal reminiscences which illustrate David Cecil's attitude to his work – one my own and one told me by a travelling-companion who shared a wagon-lit with him on the Simplon-Orient Express, bound for Venice.

The friend had the upper berth, and he says that all night long, till they reached the frontier at Domodossola, he heard David Cecil's pen scratching away, accompanied by many sighs and groans from the effort of composition.

At Domodossola, the customs (it was in the days of Mussolini) paid them a visit, and after some questioning confiscated David Cecil's reference books and papers which he needed for writing *The Stricken Deer*. It was a week before they were returned to him, but he did not seem at all perturbed during the interval. The paper he was actually writing they did not take, and his friend discovered that in all those hours of nocturnal labour he had only succeeded in writing three sentences!

The second incident, which happened in Venice, also illustrates his seeming indifference to the fate of his work, once it had been done: it was enough that he had written it.

He left part of the manuscript of *The Stricken Deer* on the terracotta stove which heated the sitting room. When we came back from lunch there lay the manuscript, charred not quite to a cinder, but almost to the point of being indecipherable. David Cecil did not apostrophize the stove as Sir Isaac Newton might have – 'Oh Stove, Stove, thou little knowest what mischief thou hast done': he made no to-do when he saw the work of months apparently obliterated. He had done the work; Fate had undone it; and he seemed content to have it so. The effort he had put into it meant more to him, in the way of spiritual satisfaction, than the loss meant, in terms of grievous disappointment. Happily for him and for his readers the ruins were not so irretrievable as they looked at the time and as they would have been, half an hour later.

It is said that Cézanne took no further interest in his pictures after he had finished them, and perhaps this is a sign of many a true artist, and one which David Cecil can also claim – that it is the labour he has put into a work, not the fate of the work itself, which matters most to him. But his delicate and sure touch on the pulse of literature matters to us, and I hope will continue to delight us, for many years to come.

David as Tutor

RACHEL TRICKETT

Miss Rachel Trickett has been Principal of St Hugh's
College, Oxford since 1973. Soon after going up
to Oxford (LMH) in 1942 she met David and remained a
constant and much loved friend to both David
and Rachel for the rest of their lives.

IN Michaelmas Term 1943 my tutor asked me if there was anyone in particular I would like to teach me for the eighteenth century. At this stage in the war women undergraduates were unusually lucky, having the choice of a whole range of tutors whose own pupils were in the Forces and who were eager to teach others. I had spent that same term on Shakespeare with Roy Ridley at Balliol, popularly supposed among us to be the original of Lord Peter Wimsey, though, to tell the truth, it had been something of a disappointment. I said I would like to go to Lord David Cecil, without divulging long-cherished reasons, for he was such a favourite figure it seemed unnecessary to give any further explanation. But I had read and been moved by *The Stricken Deer* when I gave it to my father as a birthday present some years before, and was more recently entranced by *The Young Melbourne*, especially its picture of Whig society at the end of the century which was already my preferred period. Kate Lea, my tutor, asked Lord David who replied that he would be glad to take me the following term, and some days later a postcard arrived which she and I separately struggled to decipher. Our conclusion was that it invited me to appear on Thursday at 5 pm in the first week of Hilary Term, at his rooms on staircase four in the main quad of New College, bringing with me an essay on the development of the eighteenth-century novel.

It seemed too good to be true. David Cecil, C S Lewis and Charles Williams were the most popular lecturers in Oxford at that time, and of these David, though he lacked the fervent following of Williams, had the widest appeal. It took familiarity to interpret his accent and rapid delivery (though often less time than to decipher his elegant, illegible hand), but he made us laugh:- "For most of us Shelley's 'desire of the moth for the star' is more often the desire of the moth for another moth" – we thought that wonderfully warm and worldly though not entirely believing him; and the next minute he made us recognise the peculiar quality of poetry without affectation, without, even, changing his tone. Besides, by now I had had a year's grounding in the necessary task of defining terms, analysing details, curbing an innate diffuseness, and the idea of spreading myself over the eighteenth-century novel, at large again, was irresistible. The fact that I had only read *Pamela* Part I, *Joseph Andrews* and *The Vicar of Wakefield* did not confound me; I spent the Christmas vacation delightedly reading *Tom Jones* and *Tristram Shandy*, and writing. By my return to Oxford I had concocted a sprawling essay of which I was enthusiastically proud.

Dusk of a January evening in double summer time, Thursday of the first week of Hilary Term 1944; every detail stays vividly in the memory; the walk across the Parks, past Wadham and into New College Lane, up to that fortified entrance where William of Wykeham worships the Virgin above the old door with its little rectangular opening, the whole threshold then as now littered with abandoned bicycles. The porter pointed out staircase 4 diagonally across the quad, a small gas lamp dimly marking the entry; two flights of shallow wooden stairs to the top; the door of David's room ajar, the curtains drawn, lights switched on, but there was nobody in. Holding fast to my essay I stood on the landing not knowing what to do. Through the half-open door I could see rows of books, a bowl of hyacinths on a mahogany table scattered with papers. I longed to go in at once but dared not. On the window ledge of the landing where I stood was an ancient gas ring caked with dirt; into one of its long-exhausted jets I poked my little finger for luck. It came out filthy, and I was rubbing it hard against my commoner's gown when I heard a noise of stumbling footsteps on the staircase and my tutor, in tweeds, and a cap he tore off as he reached the landing, was saying as he came up, 'Miss Trickett – you're here already. And I'm late' – this last spoken with a sort of neat almost prim assertion which robbed it of any false suggestion of apology. 'Let me take your coat.' So off with the commoner's gown, and the coat, and the precious sheets of the essay collapsed, falling page by page onto the floor. We retrieved them between us somehow, I hitched on my gown, went in with him, and the room opened up like Aladdin's cave. There were bowls of narcissi as well as hyacinths; the files of books on the white shelves were a mosaic of colour, from old bindings to new dust-covers, and a long row of yellow-bound volumes, his set of Turgenev; on the walls pictures and prints, the details of which I can't now remember, but round the fireplace a set of white tiles with childish blue emblems on them – a flying angel, a Christmas tree, and on the mantelpiece two brilliant red, green and yellow Meissen parrots.

I took an arm chair, reassembled the essay and started to read. David stood on the hearth in front of an electric fire lighting cigarettes at it and chain-smoking. Before I had finished two pages he had stubbed out the first cigarette and thrown what remained of it into the waste paper basket. As I read doggedly on I saw him, out of the corner of my eye, light another. When I paused for breath he broke in to say 'Miss Trickett, would you mind very much if I took your essay and read the rest myself? Then we'll have time to talk about it. I'm a very quick reader.' I did mind very much. Clearly I was already boring him, but I handed it over gloomily, saying 'You may not be able to read my writing.' His brisk reply: 'It can't be less legible than mine.' I watched him wretchedly as he ran his eyes over each page and tossed it onto the floor, too proud and angry even to dare admit to myself the disappointment as I saw him shuffle the lot together, put them to one side and settle briefly onto the sofa. He said, 'You love Goldsmith, don't you? So do I. Why do you think he was so popular on the Continent?' I hadn't known he was and said so. 'I've never quite understood it. He writes like an angel, but how could they translate him? I think they liked his sentiment but missed his humour. With Richardson it's clear – the French loved his psychological subtlety. Oh, and I do agree with what you said about *Pamela*', and he repeated what I had written. I began to talk. He broke in, 'Do you really prefer *Joseph Andrews* to *Tom Jones*? Why?' Answers came tumbling out, cut off as he cut in, a sort of express-train conversation carried on against the undertone of my healed vanity telling me he *had* read the essay, *had* noticed what I said, and wanted, *really* to talk about it. Then, that accompaniment happily fading out, we were off again, like nothing more than those bursts of duets or ensembles he so much loved in Verdi, and with something of the same rattling

[81]

exhilaration. When he handed me the precious essay as I left it had begun to seem almost superfluous.

I walked back to L.M.H. in a sort of daze, and remember trying to tell friends there what it had been like. Which I am trying to tell now, with the same difficulty in describing David's extraordinary genius for catching you up into his own world without either intruding or imposing himself on yours. The relation between him and his pupils was alive and real, based on the assurance that what brought you together was the subject — literature, art, ideas — as if it were the most natural and important thing in the world for both of you to spend an hour talking together about these. Unlike many powerful and idiosyncratic teachers, David never tried to propound a doctrine or define a 'way'. His famous antagonist, F. R. Leavis, is the best example of the entirely opposite type. David had no messianic or prophetic urge; he genuinely wanted to know what his pupils thought and how they responded, and he wanted to share with them his delight in and his ideas about art and human experience. In this one aspect he was like Leavis; though he was so often written off as an 'aesthete', he never drew a dividing line between art and life; he had as much to say to you about living as about style.

The common assumption that tutorials with him amounted to a sort of mutual indulgence in 'appreciation' couldn't be further from the truth. He was sharp-witted and critical — an inheritance from the argumentative family he describes in *The Cecils of Hatfield House*. He had no time for cant or confusion. On one of these Thursday evenings when I was trying to grope my way through the various meanings of nature in the eighteenth century, he said: 'Let's try to put it briefly. At the beginning of the period nature meant what we tend towards. So, if I say 'it's natural for parents to love their children', I don't mean that all parents always do, but that ideally we expect it. At the end of the period it has come to mean what we derive from. So, if I say, 'He came in in a state of nature' I would mean, facetiously, he came in naked, in an original condition. How this shift occurred is a very intricate matter. I couldn't begin to explain. I don't know enough. But I'll tell you how to remember it. That passage in *Emma* where Mrs Elton is talking about the picnic at Donwell Abbey, and she says she will wear her straw hat, they will eat out of doors and 'it will all be as simple and natural as possible', and Mr Knightley replies 'My idea of the simple and natural is to have the table spread in the dining room.' There you have it – she's the pre-romantic; he's the Augustan.'

What could epitomize more brilliantly a whole complicated development in the history of thought? When, years later, I reminded him of this, he said characteristically, 'I expect Desmond (his father-in-law) gave me that.' But though Desmond MacCarthy might have pointed out to him the passage in *Emma* he was unlikely to have applied it with David's tutorial wit and illumination. David had an exceptional gift for epitome. When we were talking he would suddenly snatch down a book and read out a passage that seemed to hold the essence of what he had been trying to communicate. On Augustan poetry and its lapidary public style, he read out to me these lines from Dryden's *To the Memory of Mr Oldham*, in his swift, intense but unemotional way:

> Thy brows with ivy and with laurel crowned,
> But Fate and gloomy night encompass thee around.

Much later when I was sharing a class with him for which he had chosen Arnold's 'touchstones' as a topic, he asked me for one for Augustan verse and I repeated these lines. 'But that's wonderful', he said. 'Not just the style; the Virgilian pathos, the tone. Why didn't I think of that?' 'You did,' I reminded him, 'and read it to me twenty years ago.' That was the secret of David's genius as a tutor, as of his genius in friendship; it was always a matter of free exchange, of mutual give and take.

The wonderful term over, I learned later in the summer that, as the war was clearly at its turning point, anyone who proposed to teach was to be allowed a third year to finish the full syllabus. The only cloud on my pleasure in this was that it would have to be a year taken up with the language papers I had dropped for the shortened Honours course. I met David in the Broad and told him about it, and he said 'Why don't you come from time to time and revise with me?', and so in Hilary Term 1945 it was back to staircase 4 in the main quad again, and the familiar room, and talk on everything. Hopkins: 'Have you been to Binsey yet?'; good second rate poetry – public poetry: *Toll for the Brave, Hohenlinden*; then Byron, and though we talked about *Don Juan* and *Childe Harold* what he took down from the shelves and read to me were the verses from *Lines on Lady Byron*:

It is not in the storm or in the strife
We feel benumbed and wish to be no more,
But in the after-silence on the shore
When all is lost except a little life.

When, a few years later I read Ruskin on Byron's genius for honest statement, and his sort of unique simplicity, it was these lines I remembered at once, though I have not seen or heard them quoted except by David. We talked, too, about hymns and about Herbert, and the importance of his faith which was always an intensely private matter to David, revealed itself obliquely but unmistakeably. He found the sweetness and simplicity, and the intricate intellectual sophistication of Herbert immediately sympathetic, and could convey this as easily as his love of Jane Austen, or Scott or Hardy.

When I went down from Oxford in 1945 I meant to return the next year for a Diploma in Education, but my father died that September and I had to find work to help at home. It was nine years before I came back to Oxford, and in all that time David kept in touch with me. From staying with him and Rachel I grew into a further kind of friendship. But in 1954 when I became English tutor at St Hugh's, the old tutor-pupil relationship was restored in the new guise of colleagues. I taught with him, examined with him, learned from him the practical lessons of professional life, and grew to know and love him even more in the day-to-day companionship that working together so uniquely sustains. Memories of this long association are shot through with those of a later period, after his retirement. But none effaces or supercedes the vividness of the first encounter – the sudden illumination in awkward adolescence – and black-out time – when the door that was ajar was pushed open on a January evening, forty-five years ago, as generously for me as for every one of David's fortunate pupils.

A Post War Pupil

LUDOVIC KENNEDY

Ludovic Kennedy, writer and broadcaster,
was taught by David at Oxford. These
memories are taken from his autobiography
On my Way to the Club .

I N all my years spent acquiring knowledge of the past, I look back on
those sessions with David and his pupils (and the crowded lectures
he gave in the hall of New College) as the high point: he was an
astonishing communicator. Today, forty years on, I see him as vividly
as then, standing befcre the fireplace in his rooms in New College,
wearing a pair of corduroy trousers, a nondescript tweed coat and a
badly tied bow tie. With his slight build, high domed forehead and
slender fingers, he looked always a little poetical, an appearance that
belied the robustness of his views. 'Who are we doing today?' he would
say as he burst breathless into the room, invariably late; and after the
essay had been read he would discourse for perhaps twenty minutes on
the author in question. For an academic he could not have been less
academic. Where other tutors would treat a text as a corpse and dissect
it as in a post-mortem, David's first criterion was whether the author
had succeeded in entertaining one and why; then to consider his
intentions and how far he had succeeded in realizing them. And so
infectious were his enthusiasms and so wise his judgements that
inhibitions one had set up against this writer or that were soon broken
down.

He always listened sympathetically to his pupils' views, however
immature or unformed, and never told them where they were wrong,
rather where his views differed from theirs. And when someone
mentioned that he had been enjoying a writer not of the first rank, he
would often say how good he thought him. I think he hated as much as
anyone the narrow academic notion that there are only a limited

number of writers worthy of serious study. In this way he let us form our own conclusions.

He had many endearing idiosyncrasies. Sometimes to drive home a point he would fling both arms downwards like a piston; or interlock his fingers and set his thumbs criss-crossing against each other in semi-perpetual motion. He talked extremely fast and not always audibly, his tongue outdistanced by his thoughts and struggling to keep up with them. Like my Aunt Moggie he had trouble with his R's, and had an odd habit common to some Cecils and Cavendishes of pronouncing 'th' as 'f'. (I once heard him say in a lecture, 'Of all fe Womantic poets, Byron was weally fe most womantic, for as well as being exceedingy beautiful, he was also a lord', which resulted in much laughter when people saw the point). Another mannerism was finishing a sentence an octave or two higher, or lower, than he started it.

He was a chain-smoker of Craven A cork-tipped cigarettes which he fished out of a battered packet deep in his pocket, then lit by poking the end against a bar of the electric fire; this usually left shreds of tobacco on the bar which then began a little conflagration of their own. And he held his cigarette, not like most people between the index and middle fingers, but between the middle and third fingers, close up to the knuckle. While others were talking, he smoked normally; but when he was holding the floor, and so as not to interrupt his flow, he took quick short puffs like a steam engine leaving St Pancras.

I was aware at the time how much I – and so many other undergraduates – owed him, and I have been aware of it ever since. One of David's many delightful books was *Two Quiet Lives* about Thomas Gray and Dorothy Osborne. Twenty years after I left Oxford, I tried to acknowledge my debt by dedicating to him my book on the *Bismarck* operation, *Pursuit*. 'For my friend and former tutor David Cecil,' I wrote. 'This tale of unquiet lives. With gratitude and affection.'

Lectures

GEORGE SCOTT

*George Scott, journalist. This extract is taken from
his book* A Time and Place *(Staples Press, 1956) where
he describes David Cecil's qualities as a teacher.*

IT seems to me that to the training of such a mind as mine was when I
went to him, crude, hungry but undisciplined, David Cecil brought
the most necessary qualities. Before I finally left Oxford in 1948 I had
heard many of his lectures as many as six times; the phrases, critical or
appreciative, with which he would describe the work of certain poets
became familiar to the point of parody. Yet at the sixth hearing, as I am
sure it would be at the twelfth, the words were spoken as though for
the first time, with the enthusiasm of discovery and with the
excitement of freshly-revealed pleasures. Year after year he would
discuss with undergraduates the Augustans or the Romantic Poets
(pronounced with a lisp that almost gave us a Bywon among the
Womantics) as though he were also discussing them for the first time.
He taught from the experience of long reading and examination, but
he listened, too, to raw, tentative opinions with a tolerance and respect
which, if it certainly did not accept, never discouraged.

Literature became what it had never been at school, an integral part
of life written by living men about life. It was to be seen against the
background of their lives and their time. The first task, we understood
was to appreciate the author's intentions. Then we might be the better
able to criticize his achievements. But the subject was approached with
the enthusiasm of the lover, not the probing, scraping, chiselling
attitude of the psychologist. The lover, however, was articulate; he
cherished language and protected it from the depredations of coarse
minds. 'You can't talk about a *lovely* meal.' He also was a lover with
his eyes open to the fact that virtues are always accompanied by
defects. David Cecil led the minds of his pupils into discovery; he

[87]

seemed to open up their minds, to free their imaginations from the prisons into which their environments had cast them; he taught them to discard old prejudices and fixed habits of thought so that they might come, as he did, fresh to the task of sympathy and appreciation with a piece of literature. It may be that these are but the foundations for critical judgement; that from there one must advance to the use of other tools; the microscope, the surgeon's knife and the psychologist's text-books. But the foundations come first and I, at any rate, was grateful to have such a man to teach me the laying of them.

David Cecil at six months old with his sisters, Moucher and Mima, his mother and his brother Bobbety.

David Cecil in the family car at Cranborne.

Talking to his mother aged three in 1905.

Aged twelve with Cush.

Oxford, 1920.

Left David as a young man in the 1920s.
Below left David, Mrs T. S. Eliot and Elizabeth Bowen in Lady Ottoline Morrell's garden in Gower Street.
Below right Rachel and David coming out of St Bartholomew's, Smithfield, after their wedding in 1932.

op left David and Rachel at Ham Spray shortly
fter their marriage.
op right David and Rachel warming their hands
t Cecil Beaton's *fête champêtre* at Ashcombe,
936.
bove Picnic at Mistra. Rachel, Lord Salisbury
nd David.
ight David on the throne of Minos at Knossos.

Above David with his two sons, Jonathan
and Hugh.
Right With Laura in the garden at Rockbourne.
Below A family photograph taken by Cecil Beaton
at Rockbourne.

Above With Laura at Chatsworth in 1963.
Left David in the New College cloister
photographed by Anthony Armstrong-Jones.
Below In the garden at Red Lion House with their
cousin Emma Cavendish.

Above left As a fellow of New College, leaving the examination schools after a lecture.
Above David in familiar attire staying with the Trees at Shute House in 1984.
Left Rachel in the mid 1960s.

Working for David

THERESA WHISTLER

Former wife of Laurence Whistler, she read English
Literature at LMH and was taught by David Cecil
after which she worked as his secretary.

M Y first vivid recollection of David dates back to an Oxford May morning in 1944 – soft rain falling into Mansfield Road – a Sunday, I think. I was just seventeen, newly arrived to be coached for College Entrance, boarding with family friends. The Cecils lived opposite in their flat in Savile House. Glancing up, I saw David's long, aristocratic upper half jutting out horizontally from a high windowsill. He was looking down, and did not move. Then I saw he was holding a tiny book open underneath him – poetry, I guessed. He stayed there quite some time, absorbed in this unusual double pleasure, meditating some favourite with fine rain falling in his hair. It seems, looking back, a characteristic glimpse to bring in the forty and more years of precious friendship that followed – except, that is, in its muteness. I have hardly any other memory of David not accompanied by animated talk – communication being his element. But that rained-on reading figure in my mind's eye expresses what made him unlike anybody else – the rare, arresting distinction combined with something utterly disarming.

My sister Jill had written ahead to him, to give me an introduction. At first we passed frequently on the pavement – David always in equal degree welcoming and embarrassed (because he had not yet remembered to invite me). I was much too happy and too unused to attention to think the delay long. Anyway I was aware already of his absentmindedness. I would watch him set off on foot for New College – see him suddenly stall: brood – turn in his tracks – reach Savile House doorway again – then throw up his hand in relief as some further recollection cancelled the first misgiving, so that he wheeled and set out as before. I would wait on to see if he might be thun-derstruck by yet another doubt about something forgotten, before he safely turned the corner into Holywell – and more than once, he was!

The invitation came – to coffee after supper. But David and Rachel had forgotten they had already invited Lord Longford. He arrived expecting an evening alone with them. We must have been very awk-wardly assorted guests. But after he had left, late as it was, the shy, socially inexperienced girl was made to stay on and drawn out with such warmth and imagination that shyness vanished. David could make *anyone* talk. From then on, I was asked often and David began to tell me a great deal about books and people and life, in evenings whose stimulus and encouragement made my world flower like a beanfield.

When my sister died that November after the birth of her second child, Laurie, her husband and later mine, was still in the army, so four-year-old Simon came back with me to be in my care and was made welcome also over the way to play with Jonathan and Hugh.

Because this was the start of it all, David's formal tuition a year or so later seems to have had no beginning, but to have been always an extension of his hospitality. And since the relation of tutor to pupil was pleasant to us both, it had no real end either. Looking back over all the riches he put in my way, and the counsel and support he gave, he seems always to have been more host than don, and his whole attitude to living influenced my outlook quite as much as his taste in reading affected my own. They seem all of one piece, the introductions to 'mocking Byron, irresponsible Sterne' and those others in the Cecils' home and to the writers of their circle – Ruth Pitter, Joyce Cary, C S Lewis, Auden. If David and Rachel had double-booked engagements, when I came to stay, I would be taken along, and owe to such lucky muddles that, though a perfect stranger, I was the fascinated guest of Iris Murdoch, Rachel Trickett, Elizabeth Bowen. David knew I admired C S Lewis greatly, as did he. I went to every Lewis lecture: to his electrifying University Sermon on the afterlife, and to the Socratic debating society where he beat down every opponent. But he played so dominant a solo on all these public occasions, that I was taken aback by the man who came to dinner. In the atmosphere David and Rachel created he sat unassumingly at ease, glad to talk in quartet, all dominance vanished. It was a lively, lovely evening and when he left, on impulse he bent over Rachel's hand

and kissed it – the gesture so attractively spontaneous, I wished he would do the same to me!

One morning while Auden was Professor of Poetry and David warmly praising the way he carried that out, at my interest David jumped up on the spur of the moment, exclaiming 'I'll ask him round!' Twenty minutes later Auden swung into the room, genial and didactic, spinning some preposterous theory that man is ruled by Time and woman by Space – borne out by the fact, he stated, that women in nervous breakdown neglect their appearance, whereas men become unpunctual, disoriented in time. His argument may not really have been quite so absurd, but that was its general tenor, and I remember David clasping his knees and rocking to and fro on the sofa like a schoolboy, egging Auden on to more outrageous flights and stirring me up to forget respect and argue back.

David's tutorials were mainly on the novel, and on Shakespeare (these I shared with my cousin, Virginia) – though he certainly gave me a memorable one also on Byron. He would stand in front of the fire in his beautiful New College study, reading my essay rapidly, pages he had finished sifting to the floor – changing stance all the time in his concentration like a restive thoroughbred. Then, with all he wanted to say instantly ready, he would fling himself down on the sofa alongside, for the rush of eager, persuasive talk and laughter that took up the rest of the hour.

I think his power of transmitting his own pleasure was the basis of all his gifts as a teacher. For him, pleasure had a serious value, and was the whole point of reading. His own capacity for enjoyment was immensely catholic and he was always widening a pupil's appetite at the same time that he was training discrimination. I never knew anyone who could make a story, a play, a poem that one had not read, more enticing than he did – by his rapid flow of impressionistic descriptions, thumb-nail sketches of personalities, lives and loves and his wonderfully prompt memory for the amusing, moving or magical quotation. His talk had also, as his books have, a great gift – not all that common – for simplifying and deepening an issue by some brilliant generalization. All these qualities seem to me, much as I have loved his writings, to have had in his talk a more subtle penetration to 'the heart's affections and the truth of imagination' than they ever had in print. For like music or a play, their meaning depended for half its creative force on the moment passing there and then:

Glory is most bright and gay
In a flash and so away

– all was in the interplay of impulse and response between talker and listener.

His commonsense eighteenth-century side made an equally strong impression on me. It did not at all conflict with his uncommon sensibility. He had shrewd, on the spot judgement about human nature. Good sense with good manners and the practice of contentment made up in his view a large part of wisdom. All his cultivation – the light touch, love of beauty (especially romantic beauty), the wide reading, strong sense of history and grasp of affairs (belonging to his family inheritance) – all this rested on something more profound which we did not much discuss then, but later we did, as the bond between us deepened: a spiritual foundation which was unusually sunlit. He agreed with Johnson – 'the only end of writing is to enable the reader better to enjoy life or better to endure it'. Literature was to him news – of a homeland he never doubted – and spoke to the soul.

Because circumstances had given me a rather serious and solitary war-time girlhood, yet I loved laughter, I seem to remember best the tutorials on comedy – *Twelfth Night, Don Juan, Tristram Shandy, Pride and Prejudice.* Also David's delight that I wanted to do Scott, as he rated him so highly but seldom found a pupil who wanted to read him. I had had *Guy Mannering* read aloud well in my childhood. David sent me to *The Heart of Midlothian,* and to that wonderful short story *The Two Drovers* – Scott at his height without his usual lapses. David would often, like this, put me in the way of the shorter or less famous masterpieces and these were of every variety. Through him I read *The Real Charlotte* (so surprising to one who had been brought up on *Experiences of an Irish RM*) and he lent me *The Diary of a Nobody.* He told me of Defoe's *Colonel Jack,* of Conrad's *The Secret Sharer,* of Turgenev's story of the singing competition in *A Sportsman's Sketches,* when so far I had only read and loved *The Torrents of Spring.* After that I read every other Turgenev I could lay hands on, often in small editions David gave me. He told me about *Le Grand Meaulnes,* not then as widely read as nowadays, about Colette, Mauriac – the list is endless.

But as a tutor he was very unexacting. He knew I had little time for reading in vacations for by now I was taking a good deal of responsibility for Laurie's small children. David never overloaded me with reading lists – I need not write an essay at all if pressed, and he never urged me to read criticism, except what was itself literature. In *Library Looking-Glass* he comments that perhaps the criticisms most valuable to a reader are impressionistic, 'those in which the critic – in a paragraph, a sentence, sometimes only a phrase – sums up, and articulates the quality or blend of qualities that for him give a work its unique and precious flavour'. This was what David's teaching itself excelled in.

After my degree I had over a year more living in Oxford before marrying in 1950, and I had Simon with me again, a dayboy probationer for Magdalen Choir. I worked for David several mornings a week as his secretary, and learnt, from that, much more about his own writing routine. He dictated the shortest letters feasible, never allowing correspondence to tyrannize his working hours. Then he would turn to dictating notes towards *Lord M* – detailed, painstaking political background on Whig policies, Reform, the Corn Laws. When he found this too much to bear, we would break off for coffee and David would give me impromptu lessons in Victorian history or sketch out in talk what he really wanted to write of in *Lord M* – the bond between Melbourne and Queen Victoria. At some time in every working day it was vital to him to get away into some big garden to meditate – for this he loved to stroll in New College garden, and later could never have enough of wandering through the Manor garden at Cranborne. He hated eating alone in those days, and if Rachel had to be out, she would very often ask me to stay to keep him company.

I could keep David's engagements in order – and so save him some of the many dictated letters that began 'Alas!' But I knew all the time that there was another set of invitations randomly stacked upstairs over the fireplace, not in my domain. My self-taught typing was dreadfully slow and stuttering. The only thing in which I was really useful, was a photographic memory by which I could find whatever David lost. Filing was out of the question – I would have had to be bossy and could not risk that. But I would know exactly what the missing letter or crucial form looked like. I would also know what book David had been reading lately and how far he had probably got – and sure enough, at that chapter the thing missing would turn up.

After Laurie and I married we lived in Lyme Regis, and a few years later David and Rachel moved to Cranborne and we began a custom of meeting for picnics half way. These wonderfully harmonious four-some talks I leave to Laurie to describe. But I have one of those long, sprawling, spontaneous letters David would write for friends, never to the typewriter. We four had been to Milton Abbas and had some of our children with us too.

'I loved your letter — Yes I feel the same about the growing bond between all of us. As one grows older — and I am quite old now — one longs more and more to be with people with whom one feels a close living fruitful bond. I feel this with you and Laurie and each time we meet, I feel it more. I am so glad we met last at such a lovely place. The green spacious landscape and long grey house and golden great church blended and intensified the mood of our talk. I wish we met more often — though it adds to the preciousness of our meetings that they come seldom.

> Therefore are feasts so solemn, so rare
> Since seldom coming in the long year set
> Like stones of worth they thinly placed are
> Or captain jewels in the carcanet!

Shakespeare does have the best word for everything doesn't he? . . .'

David told me once that he was the happiest man he knew. I think he would have reaffirmed that at almost any time up till Rachel's illness and death. Happiness set the note of his friendship, his hospi-tality, and his teaching — and now I feel the force of Lamb's phrase lamenting Coleridge, the friend who had most formed his mind: 'I cannot make a judgement of men and books without an ineffectual turning and reference to him.'

Talking to David

*Professor John Bayley, Warton Professor of English
Literature and Fellow of St Catherine's College
Oxford since 1974, was an early pupil of David's.
He and his wife Dame Iris Murdoch became very
close friends of David and Rachel's.*

I remember once attending a memorial service, and after it a verse
came into my head, from a poem which had been suggested to its
author by another such occasion.

> Ah yes, our friend is gone away:
> In sign whereof he leaves no trace.
> A perfect stranger here today
> Already takes his place.

Alas, that is the feeling one often gets from memorial services, and
from obituaries too. There seems a strange gap between the persons
one had known and loved and the devotional commentaries about
them. Not that the devotion is in any way insincere, or the
commentaries misleading, but there is bound to be a kind of
incongruity between the happy private relationship that one has had
with living persons, and the sense of general loss that comes after their
death. That incongruity has seemed to me particularly strong in the
case of David, for as the days pass I find it harder and harder to believe
he is dead at all. The incongruity I speak of would have amused him
very much. It was just the kind of thing he liked to notice and to laugh
about, and I can hear him doing so now.

In fact almost everything I think of I want to share with David, and
feel that I am sharing it: that is why he seems so specially alive. On
walks at Cranborne or Oxford he used to stop suddenly when we were
strolling along together and begin to explain a thought that had just

come to him, often holding his hands clasped before him in an abstracted way, and twiddling his long thumbs. It was sometimes quite difficult to get him going again. The way he laughed went with the abstraction too; and sometimes laughter would galvanise him into starting off again, with a little jerk, until an afterthought struck him and he would once more come to an abrupt halt. Going along in this way we were once talking of *Anna Karenina*, and of Tolstoy's unerring sense of what matters in life: a sense often quite at odds with what Tolstoy thought life should be all about, and how one should lead it. We recalled the moment near the end when Anna is going in a cab to the railway station, where she will throw herself under a train. Anna, we agreed, is a creature of impulse: if something had distracted her she might not have done it, or she might have done it later, or she and Vronsky might have made it up and lived happily together again, at least for a bit. 'But Tolstoy says that however he tried to work things out the book always ended with Anna under the train. She took charge of things and did it herself.' 'Well he would say that, wouldn't he; but isn't he good at accidentally revealing how not at all inevitable "inevitable" things are?' 'He has separate and incompatible truths, like life itself?' 'Anna is both a doomed person and a person who's not doomed at all, but gay and impulsive – might have been a grandmother don't you think? – a delightful grandmother . . .'

So we meandered on, sometimes surprising the cows if we were on our walk at Cranborne, the cows expecting human beings to move in a more regular and predictable fashion. David never seemed to notice things much on walks, but if you looked at something he would look at it too, and then come out with some new thought which the thing had indirectly suggested. On this occasion I was looking at the green weeds waving about in the stream, and he suddenly said 'Then there's that hairdresser'. 'Hairdresser?' 'Yes, do you remember, Anna sees a comic name above a hairdresser's shop as she's going in the cab to the station' 'I don't remember the name'. 'Nor do I but it's funny in some way, and Anna thinks 'I'll tell him that' – meaning Vronsky – and then she remembers they've quarrelled and where she's going' . . . 'And she won't be able to tell him?' 'Yes, and looking forward to telling your partner something funny is one of the real treats – Rachel and I always feel that'. 'The small comforting things'. 'Yes, isn't it Tyutkin? – something like that. "*Je me fais coiffer par Tyutkin*" . . .' 'Doesn't sound particularly funny does it?' 'No, the name doesn't sound funny to us but Tolstoy makes you think it was a joke they might have shared'. 'Aldous Huxley says that different names sound funny in different languages – Popoff doesn't sound funny to Russians'. 'No, there's probably a grave tragic character in Dostoevsky or someone called Popoff' . . .

And so on. To recall conversations with David is so easy, and so delightful, because they still seem to be going on in one's mind, and one can hear his voice. Another time, on a fine quiet autumn evening, I heard an odd little voice in the grass beside the path and asked David if it could be a hedge-cricket, as in Keats's *Ode to Autumn*. He stopped at once, intertwined his thumbs, and began to think. 'Hedge-cricket? Yes. "Hedge-crickets sing" . . . with the swallows. Keats would probably have been good at cricket. Very athletic – hit a butcher-boy on the nose once didn't he? I remember a friend – rather earnest lady – played golf (David always pronounced it 'goff') – and when we were driving once we passed one and she said "Quite a goff-course". Another time she said: "I must be frank, I like fresh fish".'

Walking in the garden at New College David talked in much the same way but with rather more of an Oxford slant. He claimed that the only Spoonerism Warden Spooner had really and genuinely produced was just after the first war, when he looked out of the window in the Warden's lodgings and saw an undergraduate in the quad whose face was familiar. He went down and said to him: 'Now tell me, was it you or your brother who was killed in the war?' 'I see just what he meant', said David. Dons and their ways were always a source of amusement to him. He himself never tried to be clever, or talked for effect, but he loved to feel himself among intellectual people and to take his own kind of part in their discussions. He had once been in a conversation after dinner in All Souls where the philosophers present – Isaiah Berlin, Herbert Hart, Freddy Ayer – started arguing about the nature of reality. Could objects be said to be real if they were imitations of what they represented? What status in the order of reality had toys? On a model railway you could have toy stations and toy porters, but could the porters be reproduced as drinking toy beer? David was enchanted by this display of donnish ingenuity, and said it made him feel proud to be in a place of learning where such discussions took place. 'Ah, *toy beer*', David would say ecstatically, clasping his hands: and toy beer became a sort of talisman between us in the context of academic freedom and enjoyment.

Enjoyment was the keynote in David's attitude to talking and reading. He never praised a book he had not enjoyed. In that spirit he used to ask what one had been reading lately. Once, a long time ago, he asked me that question, and I could only call to mind a novel I had taken out of the public library where my parents lived. It was called *Jane and Prudence* by Barbara Pym. I had enjoyed it, so I mentioned the name to David, without thinking he would remember it. I was astonished when he later talked about the novelist with the greatest enthusiasm and got every one of her novels as it came out. Later still he was able to rehabilitate her, when in the sixties she could get nothing published, by praising her in the *TLS*, in a feature about underrated and overrated books. Coincidentally Philip Larkin also praised her in the same piece as the most underrated novelist of her generation, and as a result her reputation rose and has never diminished. David got to know her, and in the diary that was published after her death she records having tea in the drawing-room with the green walls at Red Lion House, and how easy David and Rachel were to talk to.

They were indeed. Drinks in the green drawing-room before lunch or dinner were always a delightful time, and I remember wondering that though quite a lot was drunk amid the pleasures of discussion – David absently swigging his favourite mixed vermouth – it never seemed to affect the lucidity of our chats. Perhaps I was wrong. There were things one wanted to tell him and things one wanted to hear from him again and again. Nowhere else have I ever felt that talking was such a delightful thing in itself. With no one else have I ever had the feeling, as I do all the time still, of 'I'll tell him that'. All David's friends must know the feeling, just as everyone who reads Tolstoy recognises things so true they already seem to know them. David's intellect and speech were completely open and unexclusive – an extremely rare thing in academic circles. He never gave the impression that any of his thoughts belonged to him. And now in a sense they belong to us all. He loved Kilvert's Diaries, and on Kilvert's gravestone in the village of Bredwardine where he was Rector is carved a text from Hebrews: 'He being dead yet speaketh'.

My wife, Iris Murdoch, shared for more thirty years in the same relationship with David. She has reminded me that on our walks at Cranborne she and Rachel were sometimes brought to a halt when David and I were in front of them. If Iris was walking with David she kept up a steady philosopher's pace, as it were; and David, who much enjoyed amicable and extended arguments with her, would conform; whereas he and I, jumping about from one topic to another, seemed more naturally to move in fits and starts. Iris had a great admiration for what she called David's lucid logical commonsense; the way he instantly siezed the essential nub of an argument; his equable indifference to all kinds of cant and fashionable received opinion. She used to say that he expressed himself as clearly and concisely as an 18th century philosopher like Locke or Hume.

We always listened to him together if he took part in 'Any Questions' on the wireless, when the programme was taking place at Salisbury. Without the least intention of doing so David showed up the pretensions of the other participants, their ways of protecting themselves and ignoring anything inconvenient to them. Where they took refuge in smokescreen phrases like 'At the end of the day', and 'I'm quite sure in my own mind' (where else would they be quite sure, David used to say) he stuck to the point trenchantly but with tact. He never said anything wounding, and he stopped at once when he had nothing more to say on the topic, while so many other participants drifted vagely on into irrelevance or self-advertisement. He and Malcolm Muggeridge were like a breath of fresh air on the programme. I also used to take pleasure in noticing that David talked in just the same way that he used to in tutorials: always receptive to another point of view, always going straight to the heart of the matter, with no time wasted on inessentials.

Iris did not want to write a piece herself, but she asked me to say how enormously she admires David's style. She often read and returned to his books and we sometimes read them together. As a fellow writer she appreciated the very great trouble he took to get things right, to make his words as simple, as lively, and above all as communicative as possible. She herself made a distinction in one of her essays between what she called opaque writing, on which the eye rests; and transparent writing, when we seem to look at the subject as through a window. She said she always enjoyed looking through David's window, and seeing all the things he loved so clearly on the other side.

A Close Colleague's Assessment

Isaiah Berlin OM, *philosopher,*
Fellow of All Souls. Former President now
Hon. Fellow of Wolfson College, Oxford, he was a very
great friend and colleague from 1938.

LORD DAVID CECIL was born the second son of the fourth Marquess of Salisbury, and spent his boyhood and much of his youth at the family house at Hatfield. His earliest memories, as a boy, were of a house full of talk, sharp, articulate, amusing – he spoke of the atmosphere of total freedom and spontaneity in which everything was discussed at his parents' hospitable table, in particular, as was very often the case, when his uncles, the political sons of the great Victorian Prime Minister, Robert and Hugh, and the future Bishop of Exeter, William, were present. Politics, history, religion, stories about the behaviour of British cabinets, episodes in Parliament, serious and comical, elaborate analyses of the personal relations of public personalities – all this was part of the daily pabulum of this famous and dominant clan. When, as he often did, their cousin the Prime Minister, Arthur Balfour, came to stay, the talk became particularly lively and vehement and indiscreet and intimate – interspersed with discussions of moral and religious principles and issues – with the result that David Cecil's naturally keen and eager mind and wit developed early, and he acquired opinions, capacity for clear and articulate expression, and a tendency to relate abstract ideas to the vicissitudes of public, social and personal lives, and the interplay of individual characters and doctrines to their public environment and their place in history – all this as a naturally uninhibited process. Books were everywhere, prose and poetry, he read them at odd moments, at various times, in no particular order, and so became familiar with Clarendon, Dickens, Spenser, Shakespeare, Jane Austen, Carlyle, Lamb, Byron, Shelley, Macaulay, Disraeli; he had absorbed volumes or chapters or fragments of these writings by the time he went to Eton. He had, as a schoolboy, from all evidence, unusual charm and ease of manner, intellectual gaiety and delight in human gifts and foibles. But he was a bookish boy, and this did not stand him in particularly good stead at Eton. He told me that he did not like his years there. His contemporary, Edward Sackville-West, later a well-known musical critic, said that Cecil truly blossomed only when he left Eton and came to Oxford, and entered Christ Church. The strongest cultural influence on him at Eton was probably that of Aldous Huxley, who was a temporary master at that school during the First World War, and opened his eyes to realms of poetry which were new to him; his love of English poetry, particularly Christian poetry, stayed with him for the rest of his life. At Oxford Cecil became deeply interested in English history, particularly the Stuarts and the rise of the Tory Party with which his family's fortunes were so deeply bound up – this was strongly encouraged by his learned and sensitive history tutor, Keith Feiling, who thought him one of the cleverest as well as the most attractive undergraduates he had ever known. And indeed, Cecil's reputation for natural charm, combined with a very sharp and nimble intelligence, both clear- and hard-headed, critical both of what he read and what he wrote, and an unflagging interest in people (more than ideas), imagination (more than intellect), characterized him at all times.

He was always conscious of his origins and his social position in the hierarchical structure of British society. He once said that it was difficult for English aristocrats to be original artists or writers because, unless their circumstances were very unusual, then tended to be brought up to be all things to all men, and this, he thought, was an obstacle to the withdrawal and concentration needed for original artistic creation – Tolstoy and Byron and perhaps Shelley were exceptions. Those brought up as he was, he thought, were tempted to take too much interest in the lives, both personal and social, by which they were surrounded to dedicate themselves to hard, life-absorbing tasks. He was, all his life too deeply fascinated by too great a variety of individual experiences, as well as books above all, novels and poetry, stories and literary essays, to be able to do more than describe them and the worlds they expressed, give his own impressions, convey what they seemed to him to say and be; and this left no room for the self-disciplined, preoccupying creative labour, after which at times he hankered. After his First-Class in History at Oxford he attempted All Souls, but was not taken, and was elected to a Fellowship at Wadham College, where he remained from 1924 until 1930. He taught English Literature (and sometimes History) there – it was then that he began to exercise his extraordinary capacity for understanding casts of mind and for eliciting from pupils and making them aware of the precise content of what they thought and felt and groped for, their roots and their goals, and, conversely, of conveying his own vividly imaginative and concrete sense of what he himself thought and understood and knew about the writers and works which were being discussed. This gift for seeing in stunted-seeming seeds the particular kinds of blooms that might be made to grow, made him (especially after becoming a tutor at New College in 1938, and then, from 1949-70, Professor) a remarkable influence on his pupils, an unusual number of whom became distinguished teachers of English Literature themselves at Oxford and other universities and held him in affection and admiration forever after. At least five among the most distinguished literary luminaries at Oxford alone acknowledged a deep intellectual and personal debt to him as a wonderfully sympathetic and inspiring teacher. Until fashions changed, his lectures were vastly attended.

His interest did not lie in scholarship, but he did not look down upon the minutiae of learning, on the most scrupulous textological or philological investigations, let alone creative reconstruction of the past: he respected this deeply, and looked on as masters and personal friends some of the best-known literary scholars in Oxford at this time – C. S. Lewis, J. R. R. Tolkien, Helen Gardner, F. P. Wilson, Helen Darbyshire, L. P. Wilkinson, Nevill Coghill – who, in turn, liked him greatly and respected his judgement. But his heart was not in learning. He had a very definite doctrine of the proper aim of the study of literature, at least as he conceived of it, though he did not exclude other possibilities. He was not favourable to historical, biographical, sociological, socio-linguistic approaches to a writer, and the interpretation of his work in the light of them. His approach was aesthetic. Like T. S. Eliot, he thought that works of art shone by their own radiance, and that knowledge of the artist's life or his milieu and origins was not essential to the critic's work. Like Proust, he was against Sainte Beuve's methods. He did not care for Edmund Wilson or the semantics of I. A. Richards, or the cultural moralism of F. R. Leavis (who duly attacked him.) This was not what he wished to do, even when he admitted that it was, in its own way, well done. He thought that the task of a critic, and of a teacher of literature, was to make clear to himself and convey to others the creative process of the writer, the process of the particular imaginative act of composition, whether it obeyed rules or departed from them, or derived from examples, or was directed against other modes of expression, or created its own. He thought that this task resembled that of a teacher of composition in a musical conservatoire who describes the process of the evolution of successive drafts of a Beethoven sonata, or of Wagner's development of the organization of orchestral forces and the relationship of this to his mythological invention. This entailed a degree of imaginative insight, as well as accurate knowledge where it was available, which alone could bring out the inwardness, and, in particular, convey the specific quality, of a piece of writing, its inner pulse, its poetic imagery and changing forms which were part and parcel of its meaning, of the artist's way of achieving artistic effects. It was this wish to see nothing between him and the object of attention, and a consequent distaste for theories of literature, systems of aesthetics, sociological, psychological, philosophical, methodological approaches, that gave Cecil's teaching and his writing their particular character. It was this, too, that often enabled him to encourage a particular approach, and suggest further steps along the grain of a pupil's mind or imagination. He made no attempt to indoctrinate or impose correct methods, as some of his more formidable colleagues seemed, in the thirties and late forties, keen to do; as indeed continued to be done to a growing degree in our day.

Cecil's books, which reflect his deepest interest, both in literature and life, show that what he loved best was what was most English in English life and letters, and everything outside England which seemed closest to its, to him, most valuable qualities – a sense of lives as they are lived, the inwardness, the awareness of the poetry of quiet existence in the country, the often complex self-absorption of solitary lives, as well as their part in and interplay with the facets of various kinds of English social life, particularly when the observation is authentic, and concerned with the personal and private, and the effects of distortion or destruction by disasters or false values. His first important

work, *The Stricken Deer* (1929) is a beautifully written, deeply sympathetic study of a melancholy, introspective, semi-solitary, lyrical
Christian poet living out his life in the country. Cecil had a natural
affinity with uneasy, cloistered, fantasy-filled, inwardly rich lives, and
the deep, unquenchable lyrical impulse which they fed – Cowper,
Gray, Lamb, the Brontës (as in his *Early Victorian Novelists* of 1934),
Dorothy Osborne in an earlier century (*Two Quiet Lives,* 1948), and
this is conveyed by the best pages of *Poets and Storytellers* (1949),
by his essay on Walter de la Mare, and especially his excellent, original
and deeply-felt lectures on Thomas Hardy – perhaps the best of all
his books. But he was not confined to this genre: he gave an interesting
account of Scott's early grasp of the collision of social classes, of
conflicts of individuals in societies in flux which owed nothing to
Lukacs. His lecture on Walter Pater in 1955 is something else again
– an exquisite appreciation of the aesthetic approach to life, which
meant a very great deal to him, and which he defended in an unfavour-
able climate, as emerged in his Inaugural Lecture. Against the current
streams of the time, in 1949 and again in 1957, he declared that the
central purpose of art was to give delight, not to instruct, nor to
disturb, nor to explain, nor to praise or condemn a movement, an
idea, a regime, nor to help build a better world in the service of a
church, a party, a nation, a class, but to irradiate the soul with a light
which God had granted the artist the power to shed, and the reader
or listener to absorb, understand, delight in, and thereby be drawn
nearer its divine Creator. The true love of his life was, of course, Jane
Austen. He wrote about her during his free-lance life in London in
1935, and after he retired from Oxford in 1978: The *Portrait of Jane
Austen* was his most finished study of her. Everything in her appealed
to him: the dry light upon, and profound understanding, of the human
heart; the unswerving pursuit of what she perceived to be the real
nature of the human beings and the world they lived in; the calm,
good sense and unalterably just appraisals; the steady gaze; the light
but calculated weight; the perfection of marksmanship of every word;
the pervasive irony, the deceptively quiet tone; the capacity to convey
the nuances of every tremor of feeling and passion and painful thought
in these well-mannered, genteel, provincial heads and hearts. He
laughed at the strictures of social, especially Marxist, critics – what,
no mention of the French, or the Industrial Revolutions? Nothing
about the condition of the poor? Or Napoleon? Or class warfare? Or

the technological transformation which altered everything in the society about which she purported to write? Nothing but individual
experience, personal relationships, children, adolescents, marriage, a
thousand indescribable feelings, intimations? As if this were not
enough, not the essence of life and of art. She wrote of an England
he knew and understood, and he responded to those who described
it with genius. He felt this in a smaller degree about Mrs Gaskell, and
in his own time, Jean Rhys. George Eliot was a genius, he knew, but
for him too unaesthetic and too ideological. For this he was reproached
by members of the Bloomsbury coterie, but he was difiantly unrepentant. He was, of course, well acquainted with Bloomsbury; he had
married the daughter of Desmond MacCarthy, who was brought up
at the heart of it, and he went to Bloomsbury parties. He delighted
in the wit and irreverence of its members. Lytton Strachey did have
a strong and lasting influence upon him – he believed that Strachey
was the creator of biography as a conscious art form alongside the
novel, and as a biographer he confessed himself to be his disciple.
The Young Melbourne and its successor, *Lord M*, probably his most
widely read works, owe a great deal to Strachey; the sure touch with
which the brilliant world of the Whig aristocracy is brought to life
has surely some foundation in Cecil's familiarity with his own social
world before the war, and is perhaps a trifle anachronistic, as Tolstoy's
society in *War and Peace* is, for much the same reason; both volumes
are most enjoyable reading – Strachey would have been much more
ironical, mischievous, cruel: played with the facts to the point of
caricature, but the genre is similar. Cecil is at once more high spirited,
kinder and more conventional. He liked Ralph and Frances Partridge,
thought E. M. Forster very clever, amusing, skilful, but made fun of
their moral values – they conflicted obviously with his own religious
and perhaps more wordly ones – he compared Forster unfavourably
with Turgenev, who seemed to him equally gifted, indeed, more so,
equally clever, amusing, perceptive and humane, but with a lyrical
imagination denied, in his view, to Forster. He looked on Bloomsbury
with some irony, as a kind of sect, a self-contained, unreal little society
which had its own orthodoxies and its own experts on everything,
rather like the Roman Catholic or Marxist or Freudian establishments.
But the person in Bloomsbury he most deeply admired, and, indeed,
looked up to almost uncritically, was, of course, Virginia Woolf. He
thought her novels works of undeniable genius, but what meant most

to him was the *Common Reader*, her critical essays. These formed his ideal model – the revelation of the varieties of the actual processes of creation – the literary analogue to the teaching of musical composition – in which he so deeply believed, and tried to write, all his life. He shared his sense of Mrs Woolf's dazzling genius with his lifelong friend, Elizabeth Bowen, whose novels spoke to him directly. He thought Elizabeth Bowen, as well as his intimate friend the novelist L. P. Hartley, to be endowed with a sensibility beyond others to the texture of life as it is lived, a gift which, for him, Chekhov possessed to a supreme degree. He loved Tolstoy – he preferred his sunlit world – 'Tolstoy was surely the cleverest man who ever lived', he said of him – to the crushing misanthropy of Flaubert or the unceasing discords and infernal regions of Dostoevsky. The most valuable quality for him in people was, I think, a capacity for self-understanding – for knowing what one could and could not be and do. Genius as she was, Mrs Woolf did not completely possess that – and Vita Sackville-West, for example, and, indeed, the rest of Bloomsbury, then a dominant literary influence, in his view, none at all. He was too hard-headed and undeceivable not to look on this literary mandarinate with amused detachment, and mocked at the self-protective fastidiousness, disdainful attitudes and snobbishness, both social and artistic, of most of its members (acute even in his heroes, Strachey and Mrs Woolf) as being a genuine defect.

Towards the end of his life he did many other things. He wrote an excellent life of Max Beerbohm (*Max*), which Max had asked his widow, on his deathbed, to propose to him. He wrote about his own family and their house, first in the early 1950s, then again in his last decade, in 1973. He wrote about his father-in-law, Desmond MacCarthy; and he edited anthologies, of Christian verse in 1940, and of his own choice (*Library Looking-Glass*) in 1975. He wrote *Visionary and Dreamer*, about the painters Samuel Palmer and Burne Jones (1969), on whom he had lectured in the United States. He took no interest in 'the Modern movement' – T. S. Eliot, James Joyce, Wyndham Lewis, Ezra Pound, and their successors. The new schools – Deconstruction and its successors, formalism, neo-Freudianism, neo-Marxism, and the rest – seemed to him arid, academic exercises, or else dark mysteries conjured up by foreign mystagogues, which he was only too happy not to seek to penetrate.

All in all he was one of the most intelligent, irresistibly attractive, gifted, life-enhancing, shrewd and brilliant men of letters of his time. He confined himself to what he liked, admired and enjoyed, and described it and his reasons for it with great talent. He saw through pretence and sham quickly and infallibly. Some declared that he wrote with undeniable charm, style and distinction, but with a lack of originality, that his opinions were often familiar enough 'though ne'er so well expressed'. This is not just. His pen had a very sharp edge, and often cut deeper than cruder, if stronger, weapons. However this may be, he was certainly the most delightful human being that anyone could ever hope to meet.

PART FOUR

1950 − 1969

1950 – 1969

IN 1952, David and Rachel suddenly decided that they could no longer afford two houses and so they sold Rockbourne. However, in 1956 they bought Red Lion House from David's nephew, the then Robert Cranborne and so they were back to two houses. During the intervening years, they took a holiday house.

During the forties and more especially the fifties, David was one of the star lecturers of his time. His Tuesday night classes were also immensely popular. His son Jonathan remembers those Tuesday class evenings: David would dine in hall afterwards and would return home with that well-dined smell which children are so quick to notice. On those Tuesdays, with typical tact, Rachel would invite her Recorder Society to Linton Road. 'Ah! "Sounds and sweet airs that give delight and hurt not"' David quoted as on the way in he passed by the closed door behind which the Recorder Society was practising.

Fiona Morgan, an undergraduate at the time recalls 'It was the Midsummer Night's Dream lecture which was unforgettable. I used to sit in the front row (that meant being very thoroughly spat at) and gaze at the mobile face and the mischief and the magic as he waxed lyrical about the poetry and the people and finally, wrapping himself in his gown with an almost Nureyev-as-Romeo gesture, he ran off stage saying "Ladies and Gentlemen, I sometimes think *A Midsummer Night's Dream* was the greatest play Shakespeare ever wrote."' Another memory from the same source: 'Lord David used to take poetry classes in his rooms in New College together with John Bayley. Most of the participants were rather serious and one of them, inevitably with a scraggy beard, positively earnest. We were discussing whether all words could be used in poetry and the earnest one said 'that there could not possibly be any word that could not be of service to the art' One interrogatory word came with his head on one side like a bright bird from Lord David: "Moustache?"'

Another undergraduate, Lady Juliet Townsend (daughter of Lord

and Lady Birkenhead who were close friends of the Cecils) remembeed
a class given jointly by David and John Bayley on literary criticism.
'It was extremely funny owing to the verbal peculiarities of the two
teachers. David would begin waving his arms or twiddling his thumbs
and constantly repeating himself in his excitement – "What do you
think – what do you think – what do you think about Tennyson as
a lyrical poet – as a lyrical poet – as a lyrical poet?"; whereupon John
Bayley, who had a terrible stammer, replied "Wwwwwwwwwell
Tttttennyson etc."! In spite of this we were all infected by their
tremendous enthusiasm for their favourite writers.' Also: 'On one
occasion David was somewhat floored by being asked by one undergraduate whether he saw any resemblance between Coleridge and
Fats Waller's "Alligator Crawl"!' 'I remember' she continues 'when
David was visiting Charlton for lunch, he was telling a story accompanied by his usual dramatic wavings of the hand: it was only when
we had gone into the dining room and saw billowing clouds of smoke
that we realised that during one of these gestures, his cigarette had
flown out of his hand and fallen into a recess of an arm chair, which
had to be hurled into the garden before it was able to set fire to the
whole house.'

During these years, David published *Lord M* in 1954, *The Fine
Art of Reading* in 1957, *Max* in 1964, and *Visionary and Dreamer*
in 1969.

In 1966, he was invited to give the Mellon Lectures in America. This was a great honour. It was a high point; Professor Gom-
brich and Lord Clark had preceded him. David's lectures on Burne
Jones and Samuel Palmer were later published as *Visionary and
Dreamer*.

There are variations to the story of President Kennedy's having
David's book *Lord M* as his favourite bedside reading. An authentic
account follows: David was sitting next to an American woman at
dinner who was describing President Kennedy's and Churchill's
mutual passion for reading. It was about the time of Churchill's funeral. She then said that Kennedy's favourite book was *The Young
Melbourne* to which David replied 'That's the nicest thing anybody
has ever said to me . . .'

During the sixties, David rather modestly thought his lectures became less fashionable. This was partly because of the influence of
Doctor Leavis's Cambridge School which was in the ascendant,

although his daughter Laura recalls that people in the late sixties began hurrying to hear the legendary performer before he finally retired.

HC

As a Neighbour

DESMOND SHAWE-TAYLOR

Desmond Shawe-Taylor, music critic of The New Statesman
and then of The Sunday Times, *lived not far from
David and Rachel in Dorset.*

I KNEW David Cecil entirely as a Dorset neighbour, from 1945 until
the year of his death. Immediately after the war, Eddy Sackville-
West and Eardley Knollys – both of them old friends of David's ever
since their Oxford days – set up house along with myself in an old
vicarage in the Dorset village of Long Crichel; we were joined there, a
few years later, by Raymond Mortimer, who had been likewise an
intimate of David's for many years. So it was only natural that, as soon
as petrol rationing allowed, our two households should see a good deal
of one another – all the more natural in that Rachel was the daughter
of Desmond MacCarthy, Raymond's old journalistic colleague and
predecessor, first on *The New Statesman* and then on *The Sunday
Times*. But I have a bad memory, and retain only rather vague
impressions of the earlier post-war years when they lived at the slightly
more distant Rockbourne.

The Red Lion House period, however, at Cranborne, has remained a
vivid memory. We seem to have been constantly meeting, either there
or at Long Crichel, before lunch or before dinner, to chat and drink
and gossip. Meals at Red Lion House didn't so very often come into
the picture, because it was well known among his friends that David
never noticed what he was eating, while Rachel was inclined to throw
up her hands in mild and comical despair at the many insoluble
problems posed by cooks and catering. By temperament indeed they
were hospitality itself; only, some kinds of hospitality were more
difficult to arrange than others. Drinks were the simplest – yet even
drinks could generate a certain mild agitation in order to provide, or
find, ice and soda-water and glasses, and even the bottle that was

supposed to be in readiness for the little occasion, but had somehow vanished. At such trifling confusions it was impossible to feel any touch of disappointment: they were all an expected and familiar part of the warm Cecilian welcome, and relished accordingly. What mattered, and rightly, was the occasion itself: what we had to tell one another, what we had been reading, whom we had been seeing – and increasingly, as time went on, what had been happening to the three delightfully different children of this loving and closely knit family.

Although David might have been (quite correctly) described as both an aesthete and a don, his range of interests was uncommonly wide. He loved an argument, whether fancifully or seriously pursued; loved the theatre, as suited the son-in-law of a fine dramatic critic and the father of a brilliant comic actor; loved good new books as well as the classics and minor classics that he had mainly discussed in his own works; and loved music, especially chamber music and opera – of which last he had many lively inter-war memories of Viennese performances which he loved to discuss and recall with me, often with the help of the gramophone.

Such talks, as all his old friends will recall, tended to take place more often in an upright than in a seated position. When he listened to a string quartet or a favourite singer on the gramophone, he would stand quite near the instrument, gazing at its unromantic commercial exterior with absorbed attention, as though watching a real string quartet in action or a pair of singers responding to one another on the stage. Characteristically, he would be twiddling his thumbs as he listened: he was a great thumb-twiddler, though never from inattention and never from boredom. One would leave his company, refreshed by the joint experience and relishing the music or the favourite book, or whatever had been the subject of our talk or our attention, all the more intensely because of his own vivid response.

David As Lecturer and Critic

Patrick Garland, television director and novelist,
was a pupil of David's.

S URELY it was one of those 'talking-head' programmes, so popular
in the old days of black and white television. The cerebral version
of the contemporary 'chat-show', – the archetypal parody of which is
provided, I am reminded, by Alan Bennett's introduction: 'Tonight in
the Studio, the Archbishop of Canterbury, Isaiah Berlin, and Cathy
McGowan discuss and debate the moral and political climate of
eastern Europe . . . Cathy McGowan speaks first.' It was, in fact, the
BBC Brains Trust. Nineteen fifty-five or six, or thereabout. I must have
been on leave from National Service, most of which I spent in
Southend-on-Sea, an inauspicious posting. The usual group sat in front
of the immobile cameras: Alan Bullock, Marghanita Laski, Michael
Ayrton, Baroness Somebody, Lord David Cecil. Under discussion,
whether the youth of the present day were worse behaved, less
considerate, more untidy, than the youth of the previous generation.
The distinguished panel agreed they probably were. In conclusion,
Lord David Cecil was of the same mind, and illustrated his dismay by a
personal anecdote:

'I was in the Randolph Hotel, in my home-town of Oxford, only the other
week,' he began, 'walking down to reception, when I saw the most
extraordinary apparition advancing up the stairs towards me. He seemed in
dreadful disarray. His hair was unbrushed to begin with, and his tie undone.
There was a scattering of powder on his collar, and his waistcoat buttons were
fastened in the wrong order. His trousers were curiously stretched up beneath
his arms, so a gap showed between his turn-ups and his ankles; his fly-buttons
were undone, and his shoe-leather, alas, unpolished. As we passed each other
on the stairs, I thought to myself: "Oh, dear! Standards are falling." Ladies
and Gentlemen, I was looking in a mirror!'

[116]

As a pupil I relished those marvellous summer afternoons of discursive appreciation in his rooms at New College, where the old sounds of the bells and garden birds alternated with the new sounds of urban traffic from Catte Street and Longwall. Thirty years later I recognise – with gratitude, and with a certain degree of loyalty – David Cecil's view of literature as pleasure undoubtedly filters through to me even now. His own writing was not so much biography, although it was often disguised as such, but criticism; and the two writers who affected him most, by no means the writers he admired most, or even wrote about, were Virginia Woolf and William Hazlitt. Mrs Woolf he came to know, but he admired her criticism – more than her novels, in fact – and was influenced by her even before he got to know her.

The quality, Lord David said, he loved in her own writing, especially her literary criticism, was that she, above all, just as Hazlitt did, succeeded in conveying the particular individuality and distinction of the author she was writing about, and in his view, her essays on Jane Austen, George Eliot, George Moore, and E M Forster absolutely isolate and define that distinction. 'And, of course', he added, 'she writes so beautifully. I mean, you wouldn't take riding lessons from somebody who was always falling off the horse. Her criticism is a work of art in itself'.

I see criticism from my point of view as primarily an essay in appreciation, to discover exactly what it is that gives the particular individuality and quality to the writer. And to convey to the reader the unique taste, the flavour of that author. That doesn't mean just praising them. You point out also what they don't do; but I look on criticism as a help to the common reader. And it does that by making him understand for good or ill the work of a particular author.

He frequently discussed the dramatic criticism of Hazlitt, and how that writer manages to judge the plays of Shakespeare, first, as plays to be performed on a stage, not as texts to be frowned and puzzled over, or treated as some mysterious cryptogram. Hugo Dyson, of course, took the same view, and for all his roaring, there was fine judgement, and accurate perception. I remember always his magical illustration of the Shallow/Silence scenes in *Henry IV*, as 'the kind of history which never gets into the history books.' Second, Hazlitt relates the great tragedies and comedies to some imaginative universality, neither embedded in 19th or 20th century social or political realism

– as much contemporary fashion all too frequently implies. Where
Barthes maintains 'Society wrote *Wuthering Heights*', the tosh-horse
enters up stage left at full gallop.

It always seems to me that to say 'What has *Hamlet* or *Othello* to do with
1969 or 1970?' is a fruitless line of conjecture. I'd rather say, 'What has
1969 to do with Shakespeare?' Only the other day I was saying to an undergraduate that I liked the ballet very much, and he said: "Yes, but is it
relevant?" I couldn't help saying: All beauty is always relevant.

In his attitude towards Hazlitt, he reveals a great deal of his attitude
to his own critical writing, whether it was on Thomas Hardy, or
William Cowper, or Thomas Gray, or indeed, any of the eighteenth
and nineteenth century novelists he so admired.

'Hazlitt was an appreciative critic,' he said, 'and a good one. And
I like in him the vivid way that he writes, with immediacy, which is
always the opposite of pedantry, or dull, dry writing.' And he quoted
by heart what he felt was the core of Hazlitt's critical drive: 'The
great aim of criticism should, as I take it, reflect the colours, the light,
the shade, the soul, the body of a work. What the essence of the work
is, what passion has been touched, and how skilfully. What tone and
movement the author's mind imparts to his subject, or receives from
it.' Fortunately Lord David never encountered the passionless era of
Structuralism. I would have given a lot to have heard what he might
have said about it.

The core of his celebrated set-piece on *Wuthering Heights* may be
familiar to many, but who can forget the enticing way he outlined
the premise of his lecture? He spent – I remember it even now – his
first half-hour dissecting the uneven structure of Emily Brontë's novel,
revealing, by the orthodox Victorian rules of novel-writing, with hero,
heroine, and moral ending, how dangerously flawed it is. As he argued:

Who is the hero? Heathcliff is clearly the main character but hardly heroic,
or sympathetic, and certainly not moral. Edgar Linton is feeble, Cathy, passionate and wayward, no wonder the Victorians disapproved of her ... It
begins in the middle, goes back to the beginning, switches to the end, changes
narrators, changes heroines half-way through, returns to the place it started
out with ... It can hardly be called ideal reading for clergymen's wives in
style or content ... And yet ...

And then, in his second half-hour, like an expert watchmaker repair-
ing an antique, Lord David painstakingly put all the disparate narrative

elements back again, to show in fact how *flawless* a novel it is:

Why should 'Wuthering Heights' appear so entirely satisfying? Perhaps because it is a symbolic representation of what Emily Brontë felt about the universe. Passionate in its beauty and intensity, as well as its spiritual fervour. Unlike those Victorian values which contemporary society, 'respectable' society, held so dear, the people in Emily Brontë's novel, Heathcliff and Cathy, are neither good nor bad. They are wild or tame. They are the storm, or calm . . .

Equally vividly I remember that morning during my first term in the Examination Schools, which was for me so often a Hall of Revelation. Lord David usually began his lectures with a disarming simplicity. I can her him to this hour: 'Ladies and Gentlemen, Jane Austen' – or on this occasion – 'Ladies and Gentlemen, Charles Dickens . . . Then he would begin:

Of course one wonders why any serious reader in this day and age bothers to read such a novelist at all. The plots are cumbersome and bear all too often the hallmarks of serial writing to weekly order. The characters are exaggerated and grotesque, frequently descending to caricature. The descriptions are over-written and repeatedly vulgar. The humour is commonplace, and all too often descends to the banality of low Victorian music-hall. Sometimes even to clowning like Grimaldi, whose life he wrote. The celebrated political conscience is sentimental. His socialism, both sullen and over-stressed. The philosophy meandering and unfocussed, – pathos riddled with nineteenth century piety and even sanctimony. The female characters are two-dimensional at best, not always that, the male-characters, when they are not grotesque, the vehicles of the author's pet hates and hobby-horses. Well may we say, why persevere in reading such inarticulate and over-rated works?' Then the hesitant pause: 'Well, Ladies and Gentlemen, Charles Dickens was a genius, and geniuses can do remarkable things . . .

And of course, he spoke on for the remainder of his lecture explaining how really he believed nothing of what he had just said, but had invented, as it were, the prejudices and ignorances, and sheer misinformation young fools like myself had in our heads, based not on reading those glorious imaginative works but doubtless upon a resistance to the reading habits of an older generation.

It had always puzzled me that Lord David had never been attracted to the idea of writing a novel (although his wife, formerly Rachel MacCarthy did, called *Theresa's Choice*, in which her husband as Edward Clare, living in Brompton Square, makes a perceptive appearance) and he had attempted one in his younger days, but abandoned it. Apparently, he had thought up quite a good theme, and set it in Venice, and the descriptions were good, but when the characters came in and had to talk, he couldn't make them sound right, and his better critical judgment made him stop. But his finest writing is always on the great novelists, and although he admired statesmen and loved poetry, the novel was what attracted him. In the 1920's, curiously, he maintained there was little criticism of novelists to call upon, and he had much of the field to himself. In the book he wrote on *Early Victorian Novelists*, he was not able to draw on many outside opinions, other than his own; and when he did write about the novel, without being influenced by them, he was at his best among the four writers he cared the most for, Jane Austen, Emily Brontë, Thomas Hardy, and Walter Scott. When I challenged him that although 'Vanity Fair' in his view was probably the outstanding nineteenth-century social novel, and without doubt, the greatest poetic novel of the same period was 'Wuthering Heights', all the same he was unlikely to single out Thackeray or Emily Brontë as his 'favourite' novelist, but would hand that particular palm to his beloved Jane Austen. 'I wouldn't necessarily say that Jane Austen was my favourite novelist,' he corrected me. 'but I would say she's the writer whose disapproval I would least like to have . . .'

In my own year of Final Examinations (1959), Lord David was one of the examining body, and his reassurances were genuinely helpful to a young man who had worked by no means hard enough to merit anything better than his customary 'actor's Third'. He reminded me: 'Always remember, there are only two Days of Judgement in the history of the world, and the one at Oxford is by far the less important.'

This simplicity and good sense was equally apparent when considering the monstrosities of modern Oxford or some of its even more modern visitors. For instance Lord David described a committee-meeting, which proposed to erect a modern annexe in Queen's Lane. He had voted against the proposals, not because the designs were modern, but because they were ugly. The group, he told me, looked very bothered. It was as if he'd said that they should not elect one of the Fellows, because he was ugly, a frivolous reason.

'They insisted the architectural designs were "Contemporary". But I never thought much of that; I mean, anything you put up is bound to be contemporary. It's like saying, you can't acuse Mr So and So of being ugly, he's only twenty-five years old.'

I am also happily quite unable to suppress the surreal occasion when Alan Ginsberg and Gregory Corso, the distant 'Beat Poets' of San Francisco, made a curious kind of state visit to the Universities. It was something of a genial occasion – Alan Ginsberg was a genial poet, I remember, – and read his sub-standard Walt Whitman rhetoric for a long, long time. At the end, eventually, the undergraduate hippy-colony was joined by a few members of the Senior Common Room (I think the occasion took place in New College), among them Lord David, after dinner at High Table, dressed in a dinner-jacket. I was standing next to Lord David, when the bearded Beatnik asked him: 'Who do you love, man?' To which Lord David replied: 'my family and my friends'.

Perhaps, too, this good sense came from his toughness, but some of these formidable qualities he found within his own family circle at Hatfield, and the Burghley women, some of whom must have seemed (are still) pretty formidable, especially several of the Lady Salisburys. Margot, Lady Oxford, was a favourite eccentric, and I remember he often brought her memory into conversation with affection and comic insight. She had the most extraordinary imagery in her talk quite unlike anybody else of his acquaintance.

Of a smooth society lady, she said, 'she told enough white lies to ice a cake.' And of a particularly hideous house she'd been to stay in, she said: 'It was so uncomfortable – the chairs were covered in apples stuffed with lead. And in the hall, (talking presumably of the butler) 'I was met by a stout rhinoceros carrying visiting-cards in one hand, and azaleas in the other.' When you stayed with Margot, you'd very likely get a letter in the morning at breakfast, composed of things she's suddenly thought of in the middle of the night. One letter I received said: 'Dear David, I don't think you look after your skin properly. So few people do now, not even the Royal family, except of course, dear Queen Victoria.'

Lady Desborough, he said – and he may as well have been talking about himself – delighted in conversation in a totally different way, and in her house, at dinner-parties, whether at a fashionable table, or just calling by in the country, everything seemed to liven and sparkle. She was never a soloist, however, her talent was to draw people out, subtly and like a magician. Lord David described her to me as a piece of chamber-music. The first violin. Like himself, I used to think.

I have spoken about Lord David Cecil's brilliant and privileged seminars at New College, with four or five of us sprawled lazily around his armchair during my final summer before the Examination Schools and the day of retribution. In my rooms in Bear Lane, I had hung up the quotation from *Richard II* which seemed to me peculiarly apposite: 'Once I wasted time, and now doth Time waste me.' It was our last meeting all together, and David was asking us no longer about eighteenth-century novels, but about our lives, our futures, our ambitions. I doubtless entertained hopes of making some sort of career in the theatre, and told him so.

'And you, Duncan, what are your plans after Balliol?' he asked.

'If I get a good enough degree, I'd love to pursue an academic life.'

'What about you, Derek?' – 'I'm hoping to start a career in Law.'

'James?' – 'Politics for me. A safe seat somewhere.'

'Stephen, any thoughts?' – 'Trying to follow my father in the City'.

And you, Jeremy?' – 'The Army, if they'll bother to take me on . . .'

'Victoria – what are your plans after Schools?' Now, I remember this girl very well, although no longer her second name, but I recall still the confusion she felt in her answer, and the half-apologetic reply she made that afternoon: 'Oh, Lord David,' she said, 'listening to Duncan and Patrick and Jeremy and all the men makes me feel terribly small and rather pathetic, but honestly, I haven't got any of the hopes and ambitions they have. All I really want is to fall in love and marry and have children and live happily in the country somewhere . . .'

'My dear girl,' said David, with great tenderness, 'it is perfectly possible Duncan will get a first-class degree and end up as Master of an Oxford College, and Patrick will make some sort of success in the theatre. It is highly probably Derek will end up Lord Chief Justice, and James may well be elected the first Labour M.P. from West Sussex. Stephen is certain to be a millionaire, and Jeremy promoted to Commander-in-Chief of the entire British Army. All of their grandiose ambitions are relatively easy to achieve, if they are single-minded and work hard for it – but you, my dear girl, in asking for simple love and happiness are in quest of the greatest prize of all, and what you consider a commonplace and unworthy thing, is the hardest of all, and only a few, favoured ones ever achieve that . . .' It seemed , when I remember it, a fitting conclusion to Lord David's final tutorial.

One last afterword. This spring, at an academic conference, I met a great friend of David's, still teaching, a medieval historian from St

Anne's. She told me she asked him once if he would kindly give a talk to the Historical Society, one Sunday in November. 'Oh yes, of course, I'd love to,' he replied, 'If I'm there.'

Staying with David

ELIZABETH CAVENDISH

*Lady Elizabeth Cavendish is the eldest daughter of David's
sister Moucher Duchess of Devonshire.*

D URING the holidays, in the early fifties, David and Rachel took a
house in Norfolk belonging to my Aunt Mima's great friend,
Lady Moyra Lloyd. I was about twenty five and I remember going to
stay and finding it very exciting and stimulating. There were endless
discussions on abstruse subjects. John Bayley, Joyce Cary and other
Oxford figures were there. David loved to go over to Wyndham Ketton
Cremer's house which was full of charm, shabby and completely
unrestored. We went there for lunch.

Every year David arranged a visit to Stratford. It was very much
David's party. He used to ring and we would fix the dates. Usually we
were the same people – there was my Aunt Mima and my mother and
of course Rachel. Also Joyce Cary, Cynthia Asquith and Leslie
Hartley, as well as Jonathan. It was wonderful to go with David
because he virtually knew the whole play by heart. The first year
(1951) was particularly memorable with both *Henry IV* Part I and
Part II and *Henry V* with Anthony Quayle as Falstaff and Richard
Burton as Prince Hal. He knew and liked Anthony Quayle. We stayed
at the Welcome Hotel. Usually we went sightseeing – there was always
some expedition – and then we went to the theatre in the evening.

Every summer David and Rachel came up to stay with my mother in
Derbyshire for three weeks. It was their holiday and it was a very
important part of David's life. He was able to enjoy the uninterrupted
company of his two sisters to whom he was devoted. David and my
Aunt Mima were very amusing together. She was so brilliantly clever
and was such good counterpoint to David as well as being so funny.

It was like in the eighteenth century. By staying such a long time a
delightful routine was established. A short rest after lunch, followed

by 'the drive' nearly every afternoon. In the evening David always read to us. He read for an hour at least, short, staccato-like sentences. Because of his vitality and enjoyment, we were all swept along with it. He read Dickens, Max Beerbohm, and short stories. My mother adored having them. They were very devoted. It was very important to all three of them to be together.

I stayed many times with David and Rachel, sometimes with Julian Fane, a great friend especially of Rachel's when they lived in Linton Road, Oxford. An endless succession of agreeable and amusing people came by – either for a drink or a meal – it was non-stop. I remember I used to return to London after the weekend feeling quite tired. Rachel encouraged these friends and liked to see David amused and stimulated. He liked to talk about religion for hours and hours.

We used to go for really long walks, particularly when staying with them later at Red Lion House. During the mornings, any friends staying were left to their own devices and could be quite quiet. David always went in to his study to write and wouldn't appear again until it was time for a drink before lunch, whilst Rachel would get on with what she had to do. The remainder of the day was then devoted to various activities. If not a walk, then it might be a drive, or an expedition to see a local church or house. He was never tired on these occasions. Half undressed, he used to come in to my room either with a book about which we had been talking, or saying 'I've been thinking . . .' and then stay for another quarter of an hour. It was already pretty late. He had huge vitality and was always up for breakfast the next morning.

David and his Family

FRANCES PARTRIDGE

*Writer and diarist, she was a life long
friend of Rachel Cecil. The widow of Ralph
Partridge, she was one of the best-loved
members of the Bloomsbury circle.*

I first met David Cecil in the house of his future parents-in-law,
Desmond and Molly MacCarthy, and – although his courtship of
Rachel had probably already begun – our immediate concern was a
game of Word-making and Word-taking, an old-fashioned precursor
of Scrabble to which Desmond and David were much addicted. There
was also a great deal of literary talk between the two of them. David
was at this time a tall, elegantly willowy young man with beautiful
mobile features, and darting movements thrown out with as much brio
as his little runs of words like musical phrases scored in the Oxford
mode. (I may say that this image changed very little throughout his life,
and that he never developed the slow clumsiness of age.)

As for Rachel, she had been a mere sixteen-year-old when I first met
her and was won by her charm and lovableness. The clear well-
articulated voice she had developed in response to her mother's
deafness was reflected in the equally clear candour of her approach to
other people – in my case someone nine years her senior. In fact she
had a two-way openness of character: her interest in others was
boundless and so was her desire to communicate her thoughts and
feelings to them. I was pleased and flattered to be confided in, and
greatly appreciated the transparency which made her expressions of
face and her tones of voice so revealing. When Rachel was amused (as
she very often was) or doubtful, or a little suspicious, it was impossible
for her to conceal the fact. Sometimes, too, she would look just as
amused and surprised as anyone else at what had just popped out of
her own mouth. In the years before her engagement to David, my

husband Ralph and I twice took Rachel and her brother Dermod for holidays abroad, once to Brittany and once to Spain, and we couldn't have had easier and more delightful companions.

Then came the time when David was often at Wellington Square, followed by the excitement and general flutter of their engagement, which pervaded the house until, in 1932, what was to become and remain a perfect marriage took place at the beautiful church of St Bartholomew the Great. It was one of the few weddings I shall never forget – it must have been a winter one, for Rachel wore a little white fur tippet which charmingly framed her very youthful and rather Victorian beauty. Both wore unselfconscious expressions of happiness and hope.

Ralph and I visited them at their first house Rockbourne, with its sheets of snowdrops and hosts of wedding-presents; then later on at their different Oxford dwellings (which never seemed entirely their own), and finally at Cranborne. It was on the two country houses that their way of life was most firmly imprinted. In 1937 we went with Rachel and David and his father Lord Salisbury on a Hellenic cruise to Greece, the first on which David had lectured. We had the greatest fun, picnicking above the plains of Troy or at Mistra, eschewing all lectures I'm ashamed to say except David's own, which was about Byron, and dancing on deck under the starry sky. When sightseeing we developed a technique of taking two objectives in the reverse order to that of the rest of the party, for 'what was the point', as David said, 'of looking at Mycenae and Delos when they were black with clergymen and schoolboys?'

After that we were never long out of touch, although the war and petrol rationing made visits rarer. I remember baby Jonathan in his crib on Ham Spray lawn; the other two followed.

I propose to concentrate the rest of my memoir of David on the sixties, partly because it was a time when I was keeping a diary, and making some notes of the activity which dominated all their houses – conversation. Partly because after the death of Ralph, in 1960, and of my only son Burgo three years later, I received incredible kindness from both David and Rachel, who invited me more times than I can remember both to Oxford and Cranborne, where I enjoyed the most stimulating and civilized family life I have ever known. Parents and children shared the same enthusiasm for communicating their thoughts, and at bedtime at Cranborne there was always a lot of coming and going in the upstairs corridor, and the sound of lively talk and laughter, as they visited each other's rooms to 'darn' and embroider the current topic and the evening's talk.

David's unselfconsciousness was amazing in someone so clever and aware, and sometimes had amusing results. One might be walking with him along a country road and trying to tease out some knotty problem about Hamlet's father or the marriage of friends, when David would suddenly stop dead in the middle of the road, oblivious of whirling cars. Even when he was driving his own car he sometimes showed an alarming tendency to slow down as the conversation grew more interesting. For the very good reason that the workings of his active and intelligent mind were far more important to him than practical matters like being run over or collided with. Similarly he would often forget to start eating at mealtimes, then swallow the first course in a few gulps, and quite literally sit twiddling his thumbs until the next appeared. As he seldom noticed what others were doing, or in need of, he would often omit to pass the butter or fill their wine-glasses; but to call this bad manners would have been a monstrous libel. He was always highly sensitive to important issues, such as whether X's feelings had been hurt or Y was a bit out of things. And, as no doubt he knew, Rachel would always keep an eye on the visitors' plates and glasses.

David loved flowers, and it was he – not Rachel – who used to put them in vases, making interesting effects by mixing garden flowers and those from the hedgerows, but he was no gardener. 'This is the only moment our garden is fit to be seen,' he said, indicating the sloping grassy bank outside the drawing-room window, sprinkled at intervals with carefully chosen tulips, which looked far prettier than when planted in the usual serried ranks. For he got very great pleasure from his eyes as one noticed on every country walk (or town one for that matter), and from his ears (witness his love of the music of certain composers and interpreters, from Handel to Chopin, from Janet Baker to Lipati). But of course it was books and literature that gave him his greatest delight, and this was a word he often used when talking or writing about them. It was the quality he was always eager to convey to his students; it was why he so often said he 'loved teaching', and why they loved being taught by him.

Here are a few extracts from my diaries of these years: they at least have the merit of being recorded at the time.

April 1st, 1961. (I arrived at Cranborne much upset because I had recently decided I could not live at Ham Spray after Ralph's death, and our great friend Boris Anrep, the Russian mosaicist, had written me a deeply moving letter asking me to reconsider my decision to sell it.) David was reassuringly firm on the other side. I have no friend who enters more closely and wholeheartedly into the problems of others. I have come to harbour here – sailed into an inland sea of relaxation and calm. I loved the family atmosphere of communication last night – Jonathan wearing his red velvet jacket, Laura in pyjamas and dressing-gown. Yesterday evening, under the tall bare trees full of cawing rooks, Rachel took me to see a little thatched house in the village, that had been thoroughly done up and was for sale. It struck no pang (as I'm sure kind Rachel feared it might) because I knew at once that I could never live there alone, even so close to that much loved family. Last night, while the others were out, Laura (aged 13) entertained me at length with a disquisition on school 'crushes' and 'pashes' (not the same thing she told me), and explained her plans for making a go of boarding-school next term. 'I mean to refrain from making bad jokes, which I'm rather given to', she said. Articulacy is a family habit and spontaneous interest in each others affairs flourishes like a garden in a congenial soil.

April 2nd, 1961. I strolled with David through the Manor gardens, and that of the Salisburys next door. The serene civilization of the past lay all around us as we discussed the rising generation and their tendency to depression, which Jonathan and Hugh had remarked on in their friends. David, though not altogether an optimist, dislikes dwelling on the dark side of things, but it returned later in the evening when the subject of beating at school came up. Jonathan vigorously attacked it, and gave a vivid description of the sinister and frightening atmosphere at Eton before a beating, with the prefects lashing their canes as they patrolled the corridors. I backed him up and Rachel wavered, but it was David who defended corporal punishment with some emotion, and I was surprised at this in so kind and sensitive a person. However he interrupted himself to say 'I don't know what I'm talking about. I really agree with you. I used not to, but I do

[129]

now', going on to add that he was convinced that 'nine out of ten boys would rather be beaten than *build a wall*.'

September 11th, 1961. A walk with Rachel through green tunnels of trees. Her maturing confidence reminds me of the ripeness of a fruit that has grown and coloured against a wall in the warm sun of affection. How the whole family love to talk! Perhaps Jonathan most; Hugh is sometimes thoughtfully silent. They all break happily into imitations, bubble with laughter and pounce on general ideas. David told me he often gets over-agitated in argument (much as he loves it) and regrets it afterwards. He described himself and Iris Murdoch becoming so excited by a disagreement that 'they jumped up and down on the hearthrug, shouting at each other.'

July 7th 1963. I arrived at Cranborne early yesterday and now it's Sunday and I'm sitting out in front of a magnificent white curtain of syringa flowers. The rain has brought down a carpet of rose-petals, otherwise the garden is shaggy and neglected, but David likes to take one round it, if rather apologetically.

April 11th, 1965. Enthralling talk as usual as we walked through a sparkling wood carpeted with the fresh green leaves of wild garlic, and sprinkled with anemones and tufts of primroses. We must have been discussing the lost generation of the First War, because as soon as we got in David went up to the attic and brought down two thick tomes, privately printed memorials of the Grenfells and Charterises who were killed in the First World War. We passed them among us, looking at the pictures and turning the pages, which exuded – as all such books do – an unhappy mixture of agony and near idolatry. David paced the room telling us what he remembered about them, and evidently deeply stirred by the unwrapping of their coffins.

August 8th, 1965. Walked with David to the Manor to get a potted cyclamen. Stillness and deep shadow enveloped the beautiful house and garden, clematis and late roses draped the walls. Back at Red Lion House, Rachel could be heard shouting loudly in the kitchen to the new Portuguese couple in pidgin English. Last night we tossed the subject of aesthetes and dilettantes about for a little. Someone asked 'Would these words always hold a suggestion of abuse?' Francis

Wyndham thought it would be more honourable to be called an intellectual, but David rejected that, saying it made him 'think of hairy, humourless pipe-smoking dons in red-brick universities', and confessed he would rather like to be thought of as a dilettante, which seemed to be disregarding the deep seriousness underlying his own nature. But I've often heard him stand up for frivolity. 'I don't think it would be very nice being in a whole room full of dilettantes,' said Francis.

November 12th, 1965. Oxford. Walking in the town David deplored the terrible boredom suffered by what are called the 'beat generation' – the long hours they spent killing time gossiping around a table and smoking pot, while the girls washed their underclothes to go out on their boy-friends' motor-bikes. We agreed that it was comparable with the boredom of the very rich who move feverishly from Kitzbühel to Nassau or some other smart playground with a battery of enormous toys. I reflected that I had never seen either David or Rachel show boredom.

August 28th, 1968. My fellow guests at Cranborne are John and Iris Bayley. On Sunday night, among many conversations that took light and dashed away like forest fires, we got into a curious one about being executed! If one were condemned to have one's head chopped off, as so many historical characters were, would one prefer it to happen in public or private? David and John were quite clear they would rather it was in public. David's enthusiasm for the idea of public execution astounded me – it seemed to reveal an unexpected vein of fantasy. Talking of 'making a good end' and 'I would feel I owed it to myself', he pranced around the room like some sort of heraldic creature. Nor had he the least doubt whether he *would* make a good end. Iris, rational as ever, said it depended on what she was dying *for*. I suggested that like other intensely private moments, such as having a baby or making love, complete privacy was to be desired, paraphernalia would be futile, and all one would long for was an efficient quietus. After some hesitation Iris and Rachel agreed with me.

Christmas morning, 1970. I've woken in peace and comfort in the spare room at Cranborne. Outside snow is falling thinly. On the chimney-piece an elegant clock gives a silvery chime harmonising with my surroundings. David and Rachel have gone to early church. David is always ready to talk about his religion and what it means to him, something I greatly appreciate, but is there *any* subject, I wonder, that he would not discuss? I have never asked him, but would like to know, what picture of an afterlife his intelligent mind envisages. Hugh and Jonathan arrived yesterday, Laura is in bed with a cold. Rachel is solicitous for everyone's comfort, just as aware of our material needs as David is of the drift of our thoughts. Hugh has a somewhat different style of talk from the rest of the family — where they flash from point to point he sometimes pursues the thread of his ideas in a way that is both dogged and fascinating. I'm touched by something essentially fatherly in David, which is shown in the way he often reins in his own eager ideas so as to act as midwife to Hugh's. But he is of course acutely attuned to the mental as well as the physical life of all his children. He has told me of the agonies of anxiety he has gone through whenever Hugh was driving himself home late at night.

A little walk with Rachel, looking like a robin in a dear little brown knitted cap. Her rather vague 'Oh *dear*! We've done nothing about the Christmas decorations!' sent David rushing into the garden, where he rather wildly snatched some unsuitable greenery such as privet.

Boxing Day, 1970. Off to the Manor garden with David to try and supplement the privet, and there we found some holly with berries on it. The deserted garden looked beautiful and tragic in its thin white covering of snow. Presents were exchanged in Laura's room to cries of *'Just* what I wanted! Telepathy!!' That evening David read aloud to us the prologue of his next book, a history of the Cecil family. He read us a vivid and most evocative description of his life at Hatfield as a boy. I looked round at his three children as they sat listening — Laura had come down in her dressing-gown — and thought how deeply they love and admire him.

The Verges of Recall

LAURENCE WHISTLER

Laurence Whistler, glass engraver, poet and biographer.
He shared with David a particular affinity with the
Dorset countryside.

I SHOULD have to put top among the joys of friendship with David and Rachel, in the late years, the picnics my second wife Tessa and I shared with them, sometimes with the children of both families, sometimes without – meeting by car about midway between their home near the edge of East Dorset and ours on the boundary of west. There is a carefreeness about improvised meetings between friends who live, say, fifty miles apart, as we did. They combine spontaneity with the fun of a quick plan. At breakfast-time on a promising day, one or other would ring up, ask about the sky beyond the visible horizon, and fix on a new rendezvous. It might be at Cerne Abbas church, or at Milton Abbey, or at Moreton, or at Hardy's birthplace, or at Came church where the poet Barnes, Hardy's friend, had been rector – a different place each time, and all in that quintessential Wessex for which we scarcely needed maps. Having met, then, and looked a little at tombstones, gables, magnolia or whatever, we would drive a few miles in tandem to find the verge of a wood, a grassy lane, or a hayfield.

I had met David and Rachel a few times before the war in company with my brother Rex, who was strongly drawn to them, as was my first wife-to-be, Jill Furse (Tessa's elder sister), when she was staying with Edith Olivier. They were among the very few friends at our wedding in Salisbury Cathedral, contrived by special licence the moment war was declared. In Oxford after the war and in their ultimate home at Cranborne, where charming things were on a par with comforts, what talk there was around the fire until bedtime – often of poetry, or of personal relations, or of faith or philosophy, or of some aspect of current critical opinion. For David was as good at pursuing an idea as at party conversation, and adorable Rachel contributed nothing but perceptive thoughts, though she sometimes suppressed little yawns if she seemed to have heard it all before. David always listened to you, never dominated, always added quickly some perception from that agile mind that was as sane as it was subtle. And if you wanted his opinion of something in typescript, quite a long book perhaps, he would give it all the thought it needed, and be candid. And if he disagreed with anything, he would be sensitive, quite unnecessarily sensitive, of hurting – but still candid. For this you blessed him.

Absurd, perhaps, to feel that any of that could be enhanced by a scratch meal out-of-doors on spread-out rugs. Still, there was more sense of occasion out there than on entering a front door, however welcoming and familiar. It lifted the spirit to see their car on the verge as Tessa and I arrived – late probably; or theirs – even later perhaps – coming heedlessly round the churchyard wall with Rachel at the controls. Punctuality was no great object. So, after one or two halts to confer over a large-scale map, the right place seemed to find itself and lay out a stretch of blue distance like a farther rug. Only once in all those meetings did it rain, restricting us to two conversations behind windscreens.

The Cecil family were ideal picnic companions, undemanding, unfussy (a sine qua non), enjoying such good food as had been quickly rustled up in tissue by both parties, and such wine as came to hand, and such cake or special chocolates as might accompany hot coffee. Talk and laughter began as though they had never stopped, and rose high-mindedly above a few small, unexplained lumps under the ground sheet, and perhaps a degree-or-two more of slope in the bank than might have been wished.

Only once was there a failure, and then it was total. I must have been alone at Lyme Regis. I suggested meeting on the green beside the pinnacled church at the east end of Dorchester. For an hour, two hours, I sat there under a flawless sky that seemed to be almost supplicatory. In the end I took my lunch to the top of Eggardon Hill, and there wrote a poem (not about disappointment). David and Rachel had waited as long beside the pinnacled church in the High Street.

This little Hardyesque misunderstanding did not matter then. In fact, we redeemed it by meeting at the first church on the next occasion. But the chance of a whole afternoon, with its particular, never repeatable, sensations and thoughts and affectionate exchanges, had been lost. It didn't matter then. It matters now.

Sunday Morning at Linton Road

FERDINAND MOUNT

Ferdinand Mount, journalist and author, became a close
family friend as a result of meeting the Cecils
as an undergraduate.

A T about a quarter past twelve, we would make our way up St Giles
to the clang of Sunday bells. Turning into Linton Road, ducking
the blossom – it always seemed to be fresh and springlike outside,
perhaps in contrast to the sherry-fumed fug inside – we could already
hear the inimitable machine-gun stutter of Oxford voices pattering out
their unhasty orisons. Of the room itself I can remember little; it was
too full of people. There was, I think, a screen of darkish green, behind
which David or Rachel would dart to fetch another bottle or perhaps,
at a later stage in the proceedings, to bring out their youngest child,
Laura, then in her early teens, with all the reverence and anxiety
appropriate to the handling of fine china. It was even then obvious to
the dullest observer after five minutes conversation with her that
Laura, except for her delicacy of feature, bore not the slightest
resemblance to porcelain, being robust and caustic from an early stage.

David's readiness to confide his anxieties about his children as well
as his pride in their achievements (the latter expressed only if pressed)
seemed to me endearing rather than embarrassing. It was one more
piece of evidence that he treated me as he treated everyone, with an
immediate presumption of equality. No human being can ever have
been freer of ageism, no-one can ever have seemed less to talk to the
young with any hint of superiority or of sycophancy (often worse). To
be listened to as though you were almost certain to have something
interesting to say is intoxicating at the age of 19 (he was then in his late
50s). Nor does the pleasure of the experience diminish or its frequency

increase as one gets older.

Salons tend to become cockpits where the weak are swiftly and mercilessly defeathered. What hell it must have been to have been plumped down without proper introduction at the Algonquin Round Table or at supper with the Goncourts, or tea with the Leavises. But sherry with the Cecils was not like that. David and Rachel were so friendly and enthusiastic to all-comers, and something of their friend-liness, their security and happiness as a family, rubbed off on the all-comers. This, I must admit, had the effect of encouraging me to come to regard several guests I had met there as sympathetic characters, only to rush up to them in other circumstances and find them cold or dreary.

It is because of the generous, happy atmosphere, of those Sunday mornings that my memory first dredges up these little moments of family anxiety rather than the baying of the great lions of Oxford – Maurice Bowra, Enid Starkie in her red-and-blue outfits like some mildly deranged football fan, Isaiah Berlin, Iris Murdoch, John Spar-row, all of them jammed together against sofas and chairs, holding their ground with an unremitting delight in good, loud, rapid-fire talk. Interspersed with these sturdy figures wandered tall, thin Waugh girls, whose appearance of vague uncertainty was as misleading as Laura's ethereal pallor. It is so easy to make such introductions to social life sound perilous invitations to live above one's intellectual means. Yet what I really remember about those Sunday mornings was not the pretentious conversational games (would Spinoza have prefer-red to dine at the Randolph or the Mitre? – that sort of thing) but the rollicking good humour, the ease of the company.

As a young man, David had obviously not been adverse himself to looking ethereal in a straw boater, and why not? Yet this image of fragility and frivolity lodged itself in certain cramped brains and perhaps did his reputation no good. In reality, he had the cheerfulness and bottom of a three-bottle hunting parson. His moral sense was at least as fine and strong as Dr Leavis's. In fact, when recently re-reading one of his best biographies, *The Stricken Deer*, I felt that, far from being a Beardsleyesque aesthete, David seems almost too moralistic and comes down rather hard on the poor distracted poet Cowper. Again, 'serious' historians did not take kindly to David's trespassing on their preserves with his two-volume life of Melbourne and much resented its popular success. But was not his portrait of that charming disillusioned statesman as near the truth as we are likely to get? The fact that the portrait was so delightful was scarcely something to be complained of.

The point demonstrated by David's whole life was that neither in books nor in life was the moral conversation of existence to be divorced from delight. His character was as whole and rounded as his body was spare and his habits frugal. I was not one of those lucky undergraduates who were taught by him during a career at Oxford spanning more than forty years. But his insistence that the study of literature was never intended to degenerate into an academic grind resounded far beyond the ranks of those tramping through Eng. Lit.

His enthusiasms, crystallised in *Library Looking-Glass*, the personal anthology he put together in his seventies, show a range of sympathies neither narrow nor effete: the full-bodied English essayists, Hazlitt and Dr Johnson; the most delicate of English ironists, Jane Austen, Sydney Smith, Max Beerbohm; the saddest English lyric poets, Cowper, Clare, Hardy. If he was undoubtedly more sparing in his praise of modern writing, he made up for it when he came across something which he felt really measured up to the standards of the past, like the novels of V. S. Naipaul.

This famous gift for enthusiasm is what comes back to one most vividly as my mind returns to the slender figure cocking his head to one side, insisting on pouring out the third glass of sherry, thrusting the bottle forward with an abrupt gesture as though his elbow was propelled by some unseen agency.

He talked with his whole body and, an even rarer gift, listened with the same physical commitment – trunk, arms, legs all expressing appreciation too, as the head was thrown back in that marvellous gurgling jay's chuckle. In fact, I have never met anyone who laughed *with his legs* as he did. The convulsive piston-like motion of the knees beneath the tweed seemed to rattle the change in his pockets. Even situations which in theory should have deprived him of the opportunity to throw himself quite so wholeheartedly into the conversation could not curb him. Driving me from Salisbury over the downs to Cranborne, he would repeatedly turn from the wheel to quiz me in the back seat. What was the most shameful profession for one's son to go into? It was quite possible, we agreed, to talk with pride of 'my son the bookmaker', 'my son the MP', or even to say with a certain insouciance 'my son is cleaning lavatories at the moment', but what about 'my son has just joined a leading firm of undertakers' or 'my son is doing very well as a traffic warden'? At each suggestion, he turned his head right round to see my reaction, while another articulated lorry hurtled towards us over the brow of the hill.

As a driver, he may have been heedless. But his conversation was marked by an unfailing courtesy and measure. He radiated such considerateness that he did not have to ask after your health, or your family or your work to convey his interest in how they all were. I do not mean that he failed to enquire about such things – he certainly did – but he did not need to. In the same way, when letting fly some wisecrack about a colleague which was too good to be resisted, the effect was to suggest, not that he had been in the least infected by the congenital mean-spiritedness of academic life, but rather that he was simply carried away by high spirits – except that David was never carried away but always towards. Even to think of him is to buck oneself up a little and to re-create a little of that sherry-laden exhilaration we felt as we tumbled out into the streets of North Oxford at a quarter-to-two.

David by a friend of
his son Hugh

PAUL BINDING

*Paul Binding read English at New College where he
also obtained his B. Litt. He is a literary journalist,
has been a lecturer in American and Italian
universities and is the author of six books.*

IN December 1959 I went up to Oxford, to sit a Scholarship Examination in English Literature. Those who don't remember Oxford before the colleges were cleaned will perhaps find it hard to realize how dark and sombre a city it could then seem, and New College was more like a fortress than an institution for the young. There were two days of written examinations, followed by an interview with John Bayley. At this I was told that there would be for me, and for two others, another interview with Lord David Cecil the next morning.

It was very cold weather and of course I felt nervous. I arrived on the staircase leading to his room about two minutes before he did. He apologised for having kept me waiting, switched on the lights and lit the gas fire. I was amazed at so august a person doing so humdrum a thing. David Cecil's movements and manner were vigorous, self-confident even in their freedom, and casually masculine, and I might as well say at this point, that I can never quite connect the man I knew with the elfin figure of various memoirs. There was in his outer self, as well as in his inner, a decided firmness.

My nervousness disappeared strangely quickly, partly because of David Cecil's manner of addressing me, kindly, friendly, though totally consonant with his official position towards me, and through the impression he gave of being interested, in all their particulars, in my answers to his questions. What he seemed most concerned with was: what did I really like? What did I most easily respond to? I preferred reading novels to reading poetry or plays, did I? Why? And weren't there poets and dramatists that I liked? We talked, I remember, about Walt Whitman and Sean O'Casey. He asked me if I'd like to recite some Whitman, which I did, and told me about a moving production which he'd seen of O'Casey's *Juno and the Paycock*. When I left the room, I had the feeling that miraculously I'd been able, almost for the first time ever, to talk about the literature I really cared for, and it wasn't until much later that I realised how skilfully the interview had been conducted. He had elicited from me the things I knew about, and, almost certainly, those too which I did not know about. What I failed to appreciate then, but do now, is how the interview revealed the quite extraordinary range and depth of David Cecil's own know-ledge of literature. One mentioned Sean O'Casey, he could im-mediately come forward with intimate details of his work, as if it had only recently been in his mind. Always in the almost thirty years of knowing him that followed it was to be like that.

I went up to New College in 1960 to read English. It's hard to say now whether I would have had much experience outside his lectures of David Cecil, for I was not the sort of undergraduate who gets to know dons or who plays much part in college activities. But in the first term of my second year my acquaintance with his second son, Hugh, developed into the closest friendship. We both had rooms in Savile House, a large villa which acts as an annexe to New College, and – living in such proximity – we soon discovered that we not only had many interests in common, but also a way of talking and looking at things. It was only natural that we should meet each other's parents, and so I became a regular visitor to the Cecils in Oxford – first in Linton Road, then in Charlbury Road – and stayed with them at Red Lion House in Cranborne. These visits were to go on – and included two Christmases – until David's death in 1986.

In an important sense, then, I came to know David because he was the father of an intimate friend, and it was coincidence that he was the Goldsmiths' Professor of English Literature at my college. I em-phasize this because David was eminently someone for whom the personal life was important, who indeed interested himself in public life only if it could serve the private life by strengthening its founda-tions. He was intensely interested in what his sons and daughter were doing and feeling, and it came almost as a shock to realise how well-versed in their lives he was. Observations that Hugh had made about his fellow-students were not just remembered by him, but became subjects of his own curiosity; as much as Hugh did, he wanted to know about their emotional lives, their ambitions, pursuits, dreams. This ceaseless interest in others is sometimes called 'being a student of human nature', and indeed I think David himself has used this phrase about certain people. But I do not think it's a very exact term for David Cecil himself. His loving relation to Rachel (to whom the above words also apply) and to Jonathan, Hugh and Laura standing at the centre of his being, he saw in others their needs for love, affection, company. He championed, both in his life and in his writings, the 'developed heart', and he had a particular feeling for writers who portray the trapped lives of those who cannot realise themselves – eg Charles Lamb, the Findlater sisters, Barbara Pym.

When I was with him, we talked a great deal about literature and the arts, and when, as the years went on, I went down to Cranborne when the children weren't there, and took walks through the Dorset countryside he loved so much, we would often discuss writers and painters. The qualities he had shown during that first interview I had with him were still present, and yet I'm ashamed to say that it's only now, after he's dead, that I understand how he always stayed with subjects that I knew about and, he felt, would be of interest to me, and how I was never made even to understand the very severe limitations of my own knowledge and taste. He always knew the kind of writer I would respond to, (he took a real delight in finding you a book to take up to your room at night) and so I owe to him more than to anybody else knowledge of those writers who have entered my imagination: Turgenev, Forrest Reid, Walter de la Mare, Reynolds Price. Nevertheless I think I can from this distance make certain observations about his artistic standards.

He valued the numinous, especially when it was encountered in the apparently mundane. He liked creative artists who were capable of certain exactness of delineation of the outer world, even of society, but not satisfied with it, who delved deeply into themselves, and who 'saw into the heart of things' – or strove to, who had glimpses of an existence ampler than, and beyond, our own. Surely it is what characterises those about whom he wrote and spoke the best, from, Emily Brontë to L. P. Hartley, from the great Jacobeans to Wordsworth and Samuel Palmer, from certain aspects of Walter Scott (he was always aware of the strange and magical in Scott) to Hardy (him above all perhaps) and Elizabeth Bowen.

This, I see, does not include the writer he admired so enormously and with whom his critical position is so widely associated: Jane Austen. The extraordinary reality of Jane Austen's people – so that one can speculate about them, argue about them, as if one knew them – combined with the intricate beauty of the artistic relations in which she sets them – this is what impressed him above everything else about her. So that, paradoxically, a masterpiece like *Emma*, for all its satire, for all the ruthless analysis, does partake of the numinous.

In the other arts I remember him speaking about the 'dazzling Shakespearean mastery' of Titian, of Chardin – the quietness of whose studies has distinct affinities with qualities in those writers he admired – of the Pre-Raphaelites (whom he championed long, long before the fashion for them returned) and of Boudin. In music he had a particular feeling for Schubert, for Chopin (he once told me that he hoped his own writing had something in common with Chopin's compositions), for Fauré. But he also returned from the Edinburgh Festival very excited by a Janáček concert, spoke feelingly of Britten's settings of English poetry, and admired, while admitting his decadent qualities, the art of Kurt Weill.

Its also interesting perhaps to think of those writers he didn't much care for, or who, at his own admission, he tended to undervalue. He disliked Stendhal, and had, I think, only a qualified regard for Flaubert, finding the sneering tone of *Bouvard et Pécuchet* rather repellent. I suspect that Dostoyevsky, though he quotes the reflections of Father Zossima in *Library Looking-Glass*, didn't mean all that much to him – he was a passionate Tolstoyan. Meredith was the blind spot to which he confessed the most frequently, but towards the end of his life he told me that he had lost his former (great) admiration for Conrad, though he couldn't quite think why. He thought no book ought to be as boring as 'Daniel Deronda' and – a very different anathema – had no opinion whatever of Ezra Pound.

His comparative lack of enthusiasm for the Modernists, except perhaps for Yeats, is something I have often thought about. I have come to this conclusion. It was their crypto-Fascism (in some cases, obviously, their downright Fascism) that accounts for this. In the height of Lawrence's reputation he was accused of failure of appreciation of this writer but this was not the case. Lawrence's poetic powers, his insight into men and women's relations to each other, and to Nature, his rendering of landscape – all this he admired; in fact he said that Lawrence was the first writer in the world for some things. What he detested was his 'Blut und Boden' philosophy, his fascination with violence as a means of self-expression, his rejection of pity – all of which got him admired in the Third Reich. For David there could be no truck with such ideas – literature did not entail different values from life, and in both, he knew exactly where he stood. Sympathy, the life of the heart – here was the centre of things.

He acted on this belief constantly. During my twenties my parents died, my mother first, then, seven years later, my father, the latter in very distressing circumstances. It is no exaggeration for me to say that I survived these terrible experiences because of the sympathy – practical as well as verbal – given me unstintingly and unjudgementally by David. A sort of English shyness descends on me now as I write about such things, yet, for all his own Englishness and respect for the social conventions that make life harmonious, it was not a shyness he himself had at all. To hear confession of unbearable grief or acute despair upset him insofar as he was sorry that the other person was unhappy – his was too full and inclusive an attitude to life for him not to go out to people when they were at their darkest. And, wonderfully, as far as the other person was concerned, after the darkness passed, he never reminded you of it, of what weaknesses you yourself had laid bare, but went on with the kind of talk that had been the very stuff of your relationship with him.

It is, I think, important to remember, that for all his enthusiasm and wit and sense of fun, David had a most acute awareness of the sadness inherent in life. As a younger man he had been – he told me – immensely depressed after the Germans' invasion of the Rhineland, interpreting this as the sign it was of German military ambition. He experienced a moment of real despair when the whole world seemed to him to be made out of dissolving glass. Then, as he grew older, friends died: Leslie Hartley, Clifford Kitchin, Elizabeth Bowen, his own brother – and though he bore these with fortitude, obviously they deeply grieved him. After Rachel's death he felt, he said, above all extraordinary gratitude for her whole irradiating existence, but also an aching sense of loss, which he endured because of the intensity of his interest in others, particularly his own family.

Now I have reached a time in my life when many people I've known well are dead, and I have noticed that in most cases the very fact of their being dead has somehow affected my vision of them so that I tend to see them always – so to speak – with their last days in view. This is not the case with David Cecil, however, who is still extraordinarily clear to me in voice, gesture, appearance. Of his books I read *Library Looking-Glass* the most often, because in it I seem to be in his company again. Nonetheless I have to recall that on the day I heard of his death – I was far away from England, in Jackson, Mississippi – I felt, as I never had before, that the world had suddenly become a very different place, that it had lost one of its most radiant and remarkable members.

A Great Niece at Oxford

EMMA TENNANT

Lady Emma Tennant is the eldest daughter of the
Duke of Devonshire. A gardener and painter,
she is also a favourite cousin and contemporary
of Hugh Cecil's.

YOUNG people usually take what they have for granted. This is true
both of material possessions and surroundings, and of people;
one's family, friends, teachers and others. Only later – sometimes
much later – does one realise how much one owes to certain people.
Now that I am middle-aged, I realise the size of my debt to Aunt Rachel
and Uncle David.

Plenty of people are clever, attractive, and funny. Uncle David was
all these things. But he was also a truly good man and that is very rare.

David Cecil was my great-uncle so I knew him and Aunt Rachel
slightly from childhood. It was when I went up to Oxford in 1963 that
they became a major part of my life. I was specially lucky because
Hugh was my exact contemporary and close friend, so Linton Road
became almost a second home.

On Wednesday or Thursday a typed postcard would arrive, inviting
one for a drink on Sunday morning. Sometimes a handwritten line
added 'And do stay for lunch'. I used to bicycle round from my room –
a pretty draughty and dingy one in Bevington Road. Of course in one's
memory it is always spring – and spring in North Oxford *is* beautiful:

> Belbroughton Road is bonny, and pinkly bursts the spray,
> Of prunus and forsythia across the public way,
> For a full spring-tide of blossom seethed and departed hence,
> Leaving landlocked pools of jonquils by the sunny garden fence.

In the drawing-room, a Boudin watercolour was propped against a
mirror which reflected the garden outside. After the hurly-burly of

undergraduate life and the gloom of one's bedsitter, the room was a haven of civilisation. But it wasn't the surroundings, and it certainly wasn't the food, that made this ordinary suburban house into a light-house for generations of undergraduates and dons; it was the people. The welcome, the jokes, the talk, the fun, were unparalleled. I met many people in that room who became lifelong friends.

Uncle David and Aunt Rachel did more than anyone to keep up the marvellous Oxford tradition of entertaining dons and under-graduates and enabling them to meet on equal terms. I now realise how generous they were with themselves. Clever young people can be so maddeningly callous, such know-alls, so tiresome. It is so easy to be irritated and to put them down sharply. But, though he certainly did not suffer fools gladly, Uncle David had the rare knack of correct-ing one so subtly that one almost felt one had been paid a compliment – and one had, because he had treated one as an equal. And though, of course, his intellectual and moral standards were of the highest possible order, he was the kindest and most tolerant of men. He knew how to hate the sin but love the sinner.

Above all, both he and Aunt Rachel really loved and were fascinated by people; people alive, people dead, people they knew through his-tory, and even people who had never existed except in the imagination of a novelist or a poet. He was always able to put the present into perspective through his deep knowledge of the past. In the mid-70's we were talking about the follies of the current political establishment. 'There's nothing new about it' he said, quoting Melbourne to the effect that there are always some people who would rather die for their illusions than face reality.

Uncle David often said he felt he had had a very lucky life, what with his exceptionally happy family, his vast circle of friends, and his ability to get on with the work he loved without the terrible problems and moral dilemmas faced by intellectuals in Communist and other totalitarian regimes.

It was typically modest of him to attribute all this to luck. He *did* seem to lead a charmed life. But though luck plays a part, for better or worse, in everyone's life, it is not the whole story. I remember going on a long hot drive with Uncle David and Aunt Rachel in Dorset. She mis-read the map, and we got hopelessly lost. Most hus-band, most wives, would have become fractious at that point. David just said 'Oh darling, I think you have made an error' in the same tone of voice he would have used to say 'Oh darling, I'm afraid you have cut your finger.'

Others have written about David's spritual life. I wish I had talked to him about it, but in a sense one did not need to, so obviously deep and important was his faith. St Paul told the Galatians that 'The fruit of the spirit is love, joy, peace, long-suffering, gentleness, goodness, faith, meekness, temperance.' These were all qualities David had to a remarkable degree.

Aunt Rachel, of course was equally good-natured and her faith was equally steadfast. I saw her a few days before she died. She was not only unafraid, she radiated calm cheerfulness and her only worry was that David would be lonely without her. 'I always thought I would be the one who was left alone, and dreaded it', she said, 'But I realise that was very selfish of me.'

So there was philosophic calm about important matters. But both of them used to fuss over little things. If someone – particularly one of the children – was even slightly late, it was assumed that there had been a train crash or some other awful disaster. In the same way, both Uncle David and Aunt Rachel seemed impractical. They were impressed, if not amazed, by the way people of my age could all cook, and look after children, and even understand what goes on under the bonnet of a car.

'All the younger generation are heroic' I once heard him say. Yet his own life was so well-organised that he seemed to have all the time in the world for his family, his friends, his pupils and for writing his incomparable books.

I was not a pupil of Uncle David's, though of course I learnt an enormous amount from him. Most critics think their job is to criticise, and this they often do in the most destructive way. He had a wider and much more generous vision. He thought that the first task of a critic was to transmit to others the delight he felt in a writer's work. He said it was always worth persevering with authors with whom one did not immediately get on, because, if one did eventually come to enjoy their work, one's own life would be enriched by it. As with books, so with people. The more people one could appreciate and see the point of, the better. I often think of that generous-spirited approach when I am tempted to dismiss someone as dull or disagreeable

I last saw David at lunch with Molly Howick. It was some time after Aunt Rachel's death. With great courage, and sustained by his children and friends, he had started to write again and to enjoy life. He asked me about my children. I told him that Eddie was having trouble with his school work. 'Tell me more about Eddie', he said. 'What is he *like*?'

'Well', I said 'he is delightful, a very jolly extrovert. And he is always making things.'

'He'll be all right then', David said. 'Creative people are happy people'.

His words were a great comfort to me at the time, and have turned out to be true.

PART FIVE

1970 – 1985

1970 – 1985

IN 1970, after living in Oxford for over thirty years, David retired and came to live at Cranborne. He had started life so precariously, with appalling health, but now he was sixty-eight and perfectly well, although he continued to take great care and the thermometer was always to hand. He thought rest was good, he walked regularly and enjoyed and did everything in moderation. When asked how he was he answered 'I'm alright in myself', much to his family's amusement. He used to say that 'there is nothing more repellent than old people who drink too much.' David had been told in his early sixties that he was drinking too much before dinner. Leading the sort of life he and Rachel led, this was an easy habit to fall in to – so, realizing this he cut down. It was about then that he gave up drinking gin completely because it made him feel dizzy. He told the doctor that gin had this effect and asked why. 'Oh, senility you know' was the doctor's answer which only quite amused the patient.

Predictably, the Cecils looked carefully for a new doctor when they returned to Cranborne and of course it was important that he be sympathetic as well as competent. A young man had just joined a local practice and it was suggested to David that Ian Geddes would look after him and Rachel admirably. The relationship began well. David thought he was suffering from a skin disease on the back of his legs as he had noticed recurring sores there for some time. Doctor Geddes was invited for a drink. The fact that he diagnosed the trouble aroused his patient's deep admiration. David's legs were simply too close to the two-barred electric fire in front of which he constantly stood. What really impressed David, however, was that the young doctor had not just looked at the legs but had taken on the whole of him: for David wore thick tweed trousers which absorbed a great deal of heat before they even looked singed making the diagnosis all the harder and necessitating a thorough search for the cause elsewhere. Doctor Geddes saw the Cecils through the subsequent years, caring for them with imagination and immense kindness until they died.

Throughout the seventies David and Rachel enjoyed a happy retirement. Interests and activites were many and varied, simple as well as sophisticated. Their children came to Cranborne whenever they were able. They visited friends, frequently returning to Oxford where they often stayed with the Berlins. There was a regular visit to Queen Elizabeth the Queen Mother at Sandringham for the Kings Lynn Festival and every year they went up to Scotland to stay with Lady Elliot from where they would go on expeditions to the Edinburgh Festival.

Most of all though, David was part of the village of Cranborne. Everybody knew him and he took a constant interest in every day goings on; amused and delighted by some of his neighbours' absurdities, he was keenly analytical about social gradation and mores, and kindly and sympathetic about people's troubles and dilemmas.

A young artist, Ian Williams, had an exhibition in the disused Methodist Chapel in Cranborne in 1970. David wandered in. The artist caught David's imagination and not only did David admire his paintings, which were of local scenes, but he was intrigued that Williams doubled as a shepherd for part of the year. David who loved the countryside, felt that this man captured the real spirit of his surroundings. W. W. Robson in the foreword to the Festschrift compiled for David on his retirement wrote 'David's view of art always lays stress on its pleasurableness. But he recognises also that the art we value most offers us something more than pleasure – though something we cannot obtain, unless the art has pleased us.' David bought several of Ian Williams's paintings; the young artist's outlook on life interested and mattered to him. Ian Williams recalls 'We both greatly admired Samuel Palmer. Lord David invited me to Red Lion House to see his 'dark tower'. This picture is in the Raymond Lister book of etchings and I was very pleased to see it. I will always feel it was a missed opportunity that we did not see more of Lord David – our hours were so different.' Mrs Williams often met Rachel in the village. 'I remember her riding her bike down to the grocery shop. She asked me what I advised her to buy for her grandchildren. She seemed very worried. When she discovered that my bike had completely broken, she gave me her bike which I rode for years. I remember them both coming to the house to look at the paintings. 'How could Ian fit shepherding in as well as find the time to paint?' he asked. He was so wrapped up in the Dorset landscape. He asked a great deal about the lambing. Another time they called but we were out. I wish we had seen them more.'

A great joy to both David and Rachel was the birth of their grand-children, starting in 1973 with the birth of Hugh's first son, Conrad. They had six grandchildren all of whom David lived to see.

Jonathan's wife, the actress Anna Sharkey, was the last in-law to join the family. David and Rachel were always cheered by her company and her gifts as a singer and dancer. She remembers – during a typical Red Lion evening spent listening to operetta records – David sweeping her into a surprisingly professional waltz and calling out 'Now lets reverse!' – a charming late glimpse of his ballroom accomplishment.

What was very remarkable was David's literary output. He was as busy and as disciplined as ever. In 1973 he published *The Cecils of Hatfield House*. This was followed by *A Library Looking Glass* which came out in 1975. His publishers had been pressing him to write his autobiography. He did not wish to do this but he decided he could attempt a self-portrait through an anthology based on passages he had marked during a lifetime of reading; he was an inveterate and alas indecipherable penciller in the margins and end papers of his books. It was from such hieroglyphics that he compiled *Library Look-ing Glass*. In 1978 David published *Portrait of Jane Austen*. He was surprised and delighted by its success and modestly said that there seemed to be a renewed interest in the author. It sold more copies than any of David's other books. It was also published and sold well in America.

Both David and Rachel were still driving. For some reason, David had enormous admiration for Rachel's ability at the wheel which was patently lacking. It was some time before David gave up the unequal struggle. Just as on foot he was always in the middle of the road: so he was in a car. One day he very nearly killed Iris Murdoch. They were driving over to see his niece Anne Tree. On the journey they had to negotiate an extremely dangerous crossroads: because of a sharp bend, oncoming cars can only see and be seen for a moment, and you have to seize the opportunity and hope that there is nothing coming from either direction. David took enormous trouble and went so far as to get out of the car in order to beckon Iris forward when the road was clear. For some reason unknown even to him, he made a sign for her to advance, practically into the jaws of a large lorry and an oncoming car. The family has known the junction as the Iris Murdoch crossroads ever since and Dame Iris herself remembers the incident all too clearly to this day.

It was often said what a very good man David was. Deeply humble and a devout Christian, he loved goodness in other people. Prebendary Gerard Irvine, an old friend of David's for fifty years, has written about his spirituality. This must have been the most difficult task, for as Gerard Irvine himself says, he does not remember David ever having talked about his religion, and his spirituality was never immediately obvious to a new friend. However, even after a short acquaintance it glowed through, without the slightest suspicion of humbug. Theresa Whistler remembers going to church with him in Oxford. 'His head was bent, he was deeply absorbed whilst his thumbs were wildly twirling . . . like a windmill. Another time, also in church, during a Lenten series when David was asked to talk about religious poems, he described Christina Rossetti's spirituality in relation to her literary work. He became completely carried away by his subject and realized much later how far he had digressed from spiritual into aesthetic considerations. He apologised profusely.'

During his later years at Cranborne he became friends with the Rector, a young man called Robert Prance with whom he liked to spend time, and from whom he derived much comfort especially after Rachel's death.

In 1981 Rachel began to feel constantly sick. She had to go into hospital for tests and in August that year cancer was diagnosed. David was distraught. His courage, though, was immense. There was not a day when he did not manage to cope: although one day he had to make some Bovril for Rachel. It was unusual for David ever to have to perform any domestic task, but Rachel was feeling very unwell and it was the housekeeper's day off. Rachel said: 'David returned with a very small cup that I didn't even know I possessed.' In March 1982, she said to Laura 'I've fallen on to another shelf.' In July that year Rachel died in her bed holding David's hand.

During this long and miserable illness, both David and Rachel had derived great comfort from the Macmillan Nurses for whom he felt a deep gratitude for the rest of his life. Ian Geddes with his usual tact and imagination had been a great support and the bond between him and David deepened accordingly.

David lived for another three and a half years.

The contributors to this section describe how he spent his time: seeing his friends and his family and still very much taking part, still interested, still amused. But the light had gone out. He never ceased to mourn Rachel. Unbelievably, he wrote two more books after Rachel died, *Charles Lamb* published in 1983 and *Some Dorset Country Houses* published in 1985.

Janet and Reynolds Stone were special friends of the Cecils. Reynolds Stone had died in 1979 and his widow writes: 'It so came about that I saw David almost every week after Rachel died, being in the same boat so to speak, and by chance within a few miles. 'Janet, do come over for tea. I hate this cold and the darkness of winter, don't you?' Nothing cheered me up more – no moanings (apart from the weather) or lamentations, but heavenly gossip, and discussions on life and death, our families – which David had mentioned were so alike – and the 1662 Prayer Book we both had an undying obsession about. Tea was just flannel-type toast, and no passing. One grabbed or starved, suiting the brave, but less so, the young and timid. Not that David was thoughtless, just madly above food – or gardening, or any shade of prinkiness'.

After nearly fifty years of marriage during which Rachel had looked after all the administration, it was nevertheless a surprise to his children when it became apparent that David had never seen a bank statement. When he received his first after Rachel's death, he asked Jonathan whether he should acknowledge it. From early on in his widowerhood he had a kind and faithful housekeeper called Lily Savage. She was tactful and imaginative. She cooked for him; she drove him wherever he wanted to go after packing his suitcase, and she was to remain with him till the end.

Rather suddenly, in late 1985, David's health deteriorated. It became apparent that he was not going to get better although he managed one last visit to Hatfield for Christmas, doing his Christmas shopping in Halls of Oxford as usual on the way. On his return, he saw Dr Geddes and seemed rather relieved by the consultation. He said 'I may recover and I may die, but to tell you the truth I don't mind which'. On the last morning Hugh and Jonathan joined Laura at Red Lion House knowing it was very near the end. A nurse had already been sent for and had just arrived. Rather short of breath, David said to his children 'Oh it is good of you to come. I'm afraid it will be rather dull, I won't be able to talk much.' To the nurse who was settling him on the pillows he said 'You won't know this but I'm usually quite a talker.' He died moments later. It was New Year's Day.

HC

An Old Friendship Revived

RALPH RICKETTS

A FTER we left Oxford David and I did not meet for a very considerable period. When a large party was arranged for Leslie Hartley's
seventieth birthday, to my great pleasure I met David again at it. We
talked as happily as we had at Oxford, if not more so. I suppose it
could be said we had matured. We certainly had changed considerably
since our undergraduate days. I was very pleased to find that at dinner
I was placed next to Rachel, whom I had never met. It did not take me
long to see why David had married her. She had a delightful face with
large, expressive brown eyes. She was clever, witty and sensitive. She
gave me the impression of natural youthfulness, a quality she retained
into old age. David and I saw each other now and then after this
dinner; one occasion being when Leslie Hartley, who had become a
close friend of mine, experienced a particularly severe domestic crisis.
We thought we would go down to his house near Bath and see how he
had survivied. My wife, Margaret, and I picked up David at Wilton
and after lunch in a pub drove down to Bathgate. We found Leslie
surprisingly unperturbed. On the way home, as on the way there,
David and I talked without ceasing.

As an old man, he developed an engagingly objective view of his
youthful pecadillos. I remember flipping through an autobiography
with him, coming on a passage which commented on his vanity. Many
men, especially vain men, would have been upset, hastened to explain
or deny. Not David. He looked at me and said calmly: 'I think that is
fair Ralph, don't you?'

A few years later, Leslie died in his London flat, David and I sitting
one on each side of the bed. He was in a coma most of the time, dying
in the early morning. Then came the Memorial Service to which all
four went. It is from that day that I would date my *real* friendship with
David. It was as though a fire had been lighted. We began to stay with
each other more often; in the intervals between visits we would

telephone for no particular reason, often beginning the conversation with some fatuous remark such as: 'What have you been thinking about today?' Gradually we progressed towards the remarkable friendship of our old age. There was nothing sentimental about our relationship; it was stimulating, inspiring, often hilarious. We exchanged stories about people we knew. We discussed everything – ourselves of course, our wives, our children and grandchildren; we talked of men we had known at Oxford, many now dead, of writers. I remember long conversations about Jane Austen and the Brontës, especially Emily Brontë of whom we were great admirers. We talked too of artists, and, more and more, of religion. The deeper we delved into each other's heart and mind, the more we found agreement. The fact that we always eventually agreed might make the discussions sound dull, but there was nothing dull about them. Quite often we found different reasons for our final agreement. 'We might be two brothers,' one of us said. 'Identical twins,' the other capped him, laughing. There was a lot of laughter. A bonus was that Rachel and Margaret had formed a friendship which was almost as close as our own.

I remember one lovely June day when we met halfway between our house (in Hampshire) and theirs. We had a picnic in the New Forest and my recollection is that we laughed almost continuously as we munched our sandwiches.

Another time when we were staying with them, it came out that Margaret was to have an operation the following week. 'Rachel', David exclaimed, 'we must put off everything, Ralph must not be alone the night Margaret goes into hospital'. Duly at tea time they drove up to the house, refusing to leave till the news came next day that the operation had been successful.

David was tireless mentally. I remember ringing him up one day, saying that he must go to Salisbury at once and buy a certain book. The following day he telephoned. After three attempts he had found the book, had read it through most of the night, finished it and now was going to read it again. A few weeks after this Rachel had to go into hospital 'for tests'. The diagnosis was inoperable cancer of the liver; she was unlikely to live more than a year.

Our visits continued as before except that now we always went to stay with them. Rachel suffered terribly from nausea. Sometimes this was mentioned quite naturally depending on the drift of the conversation, but I don't remember her ever complaining. Margaret and I felt that instead of our giving her courage she gave it to us. Latterly she only came down at tea time in her dressing gown; otherwise everyday life went on as usual. Time passed. Rachel died. I shall never forget David's bearing as he stood beside her grave.

Naturally we increased our visits to Red Lion House, and David often came to us. When a visit to him coincided with a Tuesday evening, we would go to a beautiful small church at Wimborne St Giles. Usually there was no one there except the Rector, the Verger and we three. We sat in the wooden stalls beyond the screen close to the altar. It was then that I became concerned about David's physical health. Although the aisle was between us, his breathing was painfully audible. His children were very supportive and sympathetic. They were a most united family. After one or two attempts, his daughter, Laura, produced the perfect housekeeper. Lily Savage – her surname was most inappropriate – had never been 'in service', but David and she struck the right note with each other from the start. Moreover she was a very good cook. David even managed to achieve a kind of happiness; he once said to me that he would like to live two more years. Beneath his sensitivity was a strong spirit. After he died it was a consolation to me to remember that throughout our long friendship neither of us had said a word or done anything which irritated or hurt the other.

Gradually David grew more easily tired, more absent-minded. In his house we came down to breakfast in our dressing-gowns, David talking as much as ever as he helped himself to coffee. When he had dressed and come downstairs again he would, almost invariably, call out: 'Lily, could you bring down my hearing-aid? It's on my dressing-table.' At lunch and dinner he often forgot to ring for the next course. There we would sit till one of us reminded him that the food was waiting. Although we were now three, he never let Margaret feel left out. His perfect manners continued to the end.

A Television Interview

TRISTRAM POWELL

Tristram Powell, television film director, became
friends with Jonathan Cecil while at Eton and subsequently
with the rest of the family.

IN 1970 I tried to pass on to a television audience the pleasure of
David's company when I made a documentary for the BBC called
'Conversations at Cranborne'. David sat in the garden of Cranborne
Manor and talked to Patrick Garland, an old pupil of his. In order to
give the flavour of David's talk, I have chosen the following passages
from the transcript of the programme.

On Aldous Huxley, a junior master at Eton:
He had come down from Oxford. He couldn't go into the war, he was
blind nearly, and he looked very odd. This very distinguished, very
long, tall, pale piece of macaroni, and he used to wear an orange scarf
which was very unlike most Eton masters and I thought very beautiful.
And he was awfully good with one because he wasn't patronising, on
the other hand he didn't try and be on too familiar terms – he just
talked to one about literature. And he gave me books to read and all
sorts of things like the Elizabethan dramatists that I hadn't read, the
non-Shakespearean ones.

On Yeats:
I knew Yeats. He made a very strong impression. He wasn't an
intimate friend, but I met him at Lady Ottoline Morrell's and he talked
to me about how he lived very quietly just seeing a few friends and
some witches. And then later on I met him in London once or twice,
and when he was quite old I stayed in a country house for a weekend
with him. He was a very, very unexpected personality. Well, perhaps
not unexpected. One might have expected it. But a very unusual

personality. Because he was, I think, a very great poet and he behaved like that. And in that way I think he was very un-English, at least of our day, because the English always tend to play the personality down and say a great statesman or a poet is really quite a simple person. But there was no nonsense like that about Yeats. And he was very fine looking, although getting a bit fatter, he had great waving locks of hair and a great eyeglass and a great black ribbon and a huge great bow here and he talked in this chanting, curious, Celtic voice. I know that my father-in-law said to me that Yeats had said to him 'the floor of heaven is full of the clashing of swords'. A most wonderful way to talk, wasn't it? The only thing is, what can one say back? 'What a pity, or 'how delightful' or 'will it go on'? It would be difficult to make a reply equal to this spendid statement. Then after dinner he read aloud, and that again, should one laugh or should one admire. Admire really. He read with his great chanting voice and then he beat time, you know. I remember a passage,

I can't do it in his accent you know: 'And the bones were in the womb' (bang, bang) 'and the womb loathed the bones' (bang, bang) – like that. But all the same it was very majestic, and one did realise that he was equal to the poetry in a way, only it was a great performance and one had to adjust ones English ideas to accept it.

On Shakespeare:
The first play I ever saw was a Shakespeare play. I had the Lambs' *Tales*, and then bits of the real plays. Of course I didn't understand a third of the words, but they get through to you, don't they? The great rolling emotion somehow comes through. So it was personal. But I think also if you're English and English literature is the thing, you can't help it. In Shakespeare the more I read the more I see the amount of things that come from Shakespeare or come via Shakespeare to the English cannot be exaggerated, and you find it everywhere, it's like the air you breathe. And so one's categories of character are so much the ones that Shakespeare created. The heroine for instance. In English literature and for English people there are two kinds of heroines, either the very sweet, submissive kind or the spirited, gay, resourceful woman. Desdemona and Rosalind. No other literatures have them. There are none in the Russian or French, they're English, and who does it come from – from Shakespeare. And I don't think it's just that the writers do it, I think people have just begun to think like that.

On Jane Austen:
Jane Austen influenced me very much in a general way. I read her early with great pleasure and often since, and I think it's the, it's the tone is what I've liked about her, very cool, amused, but not ill-tempered tone. What I liked so very much about her is that she's quite ruthless in pointing out weaknesses and making fun, but she never seems in a bad temper, wishing to do down the characters, and I find this very agreeable – this sort of ruthless, good tempered, just, humourous outlook. I also like the mixture of her rather tough, robust judgement combined with a silvery, elegant refinement of manner. I think this contrast between the delicacy of the manner and the robustness of the judement is very sympathetic to me. And, I can't say I can, but I would like to aspire to both.

On Oxford Politics:
You never knew what side people were going to be on. I remember when there was a question of taking down the window by Sir Joshua Reynolds in New College Chapel because it was unsuitable to a medieval church. The College divided very violently and you never knew what side anybody was going to be on. I was passionately for keeping it. I think it's a wonderful window and I like the 18th century, but I got such unexpected supporters you know. I got a famous philosopher because he hated anything after medieval at all, and thought that was best. I got somebody because they didn't like the Warden who wanted the window changed, and then another old fellow who said he supported me because he believed one of his great aunts had sat for the figure of Chastity in it. Well, that was a great credit to his aunt but no special reason for keeping the window.

On the tutorial system:
I think in many academic institutions it's all big lectures, big classes – but the essence of the Oxford system is you see the pupil alone or in a pair. They don't have to go to lectures, if you're a lecturer you soon find that out, very few come very often, but they have to come to you for their tutorial and then, if you like teaching – of course you've got to do that – I find it a very nice way because you can learn to alter and adapt according to the character and tastes of the person you're teaching, and this makes it very human, and so it's a personal thing as well as the subject.

On biography:
I can't write about people I don't like. You see if you write about a person you live with them all the time and to live with somebody you don't like for several years on end is very disagreeable I think. And I can't imagine writing a biography of a person one can't enter into.

On humour:
I'm a great believer in comedy and humour as a part of truth. I think to take anybody wholly seriously means that you don't see them as they really are. Certainly I can't take myself terribly seriously. And anybody would be very wrong who did.

Tristram Powell adds:
I wish I could have put into the programme the intense enjoyment of staying with the family in Oxford or at Red Lion House, Cranborne. David's appetite was more for conversation than for food. He would briefly stop talking for a sudden rapid intake, the rest of the meal he'd spend distractedly crumbling water biscuits in one hand. He was particularly at ease and generous with young people and was always curious to know what they thought about the things in life that interested them.

As a Patient

IAN GEDDES

Doctor Geddes was the family G.P. and looked after
David and Rachel until their death.

FROM an early age I remember my parents talking about David Cecil
and Professor Joad on the 'Brains Trust'. I was introduced to him
on my first evening in Dorset when he made a presentation on the
behalf of the patients in the Sixpenny Handley practice to my
predecessors Drs Paul and Zoe Harris. The occasion was held in a large
barn garlanded with flowers and exuded the spirit of Hardy's Wessex
– a startling contrast to the West of Scotland which I had just left.

I came to know him well as a patient especially during Lady David's
long illness. Visits to Red Lion House were, as for everyone, a pleasure.
Lord David's limitless interest in every aspect of life and literature led
into fascinating discussions which drew knowledge, thoughts and
opinions out of me which I did not know I had, so that I would leave
revitalised, hoping that I had given a fraction of the benefit in return.
He was never overbearing with his intellect and knowledge. His
enthusiasm for sharing his love of literature never left him. When he
talked with my daughter about English novelists he became as excited
at reading a passage as though it were for the first time and his foot
movements would increase as the excitement grew.

His courtesy and air of not quite being able to cope with the modern
world endeared him to all. His visits to the surgery are still
remembered with warmth and sometimes amusement. He always
insisted that other patients be seen first. On one such visit while I was
meeting with the other members of our primary care team our
discussion was rudely interrupted by the squealing of tyres. Lord
David had started the engine of his car while it was still in reverse gear.
The car executed a high speed reverse pirouette, ending by ascending a
bank and knocking over a hawthorn tree. A shaken David accepted

[166]

the offer of our social worker to drive him home. He never did know that he was a retired inspector of police! Lord David's hawthorn flourishes at an unusual angle.

In his later years he did not always enjoy good health and was at times exceedingly breathless. He spent many mornings in a large old cream-coloured bed surrounded by piles of books and manuscripts and would stay up late at night talking. He was never fearful of death having a deep faith which led him to enjoy and benefit from long discussions with Robert Prance, the vicar of the church in Cranborne which he regularly attended.

When I told him that his beloved Rachel was mortally ill he was devastated. He said on many occasions that theirs had been a perfect marriage in which he was blissfully happy. He was very aware that without her, he would not have been able to make the contribution to life that he did. When they first met he was a very diffident young man plagued with self doubts which may have helped him to empathise with Cowper and so perfectly describe his feelings in *The Stricken Deer*. But the support was mutual. Initially he could not conceive that he would be able to care for her in their house. When he began to realise that this was possible with the help of his devoted family and the MacMillan Service, he constantly amazed himself at his ability to cope. When she died his deep sadness was tempered by his relief that he had succeeded beyond his wildest dreams.

He was deeply grateful to the MacMillan service and offered to broadcast an appeal on their behalf. It was written in his usual beautiful and perfect prose and he was upset when an editor at the BBC 'improved' it and would not broadcast it in its original form. Eventually it was broadcast more or less as written.

After Rachel's death he determined to live as fully as he could but 'did not want to live long'. His anxiety that, like his sister, he might lose his intellect haunted him. But he did not do so and he continued to enjoy conversations and particularly visiting some Dorset country houses with David Burnett for his last book. It was his heart that failed him but not until after he had been able to enjoy one last Christmas at Hatfield.

More than an Uncle

ANNE TREE

*Lady Anne Tree is the daughter of David's sister
Moucher, Duchess of Devonshire. Although family friends
for years, it was not until the Trees moved down to Dorset
in 1970 and they saw David and Rachel regularly that a close
friendship developed between uncle and niece.*

I can remember David on Salisbury station. He was dressed to go to
his brother's (Uncle Bobbety's) Memorial Service at Westminster
Abbey. He wore a tail coat which was much too long for him. It being a
very cold day, he wore an overcoat and the tails came down well below
the coat – it was terribly funny. In his dress, David was both elegant
and scruffy: he would take a fancy to a smart bow tie or velvet jacket
but would very often wear that unspeakable Bohemian cap as well.

In later life, it was no good talking to David without Rachel. They
were like Siamese twins – totally inseparable. Once a year Rachel went
to her Recorder Society's Concert Weekend. She was away for two
nights and it always took place during the winter. David would come
and stay with us. On the Sunday when she was due back, the shutter
was left open so that David could listen for the sound of the car's tyres
on the gravel signifying her return. On those evenings we would talk
over tea but David was thinking about the shutter and whether he
thought he had heard Rachel returning. When she arrived, he never
wanted to stay any longer. He wanted to get back home and be alone
with Rachel. Their affinity was so strong, he was almost like a fish out
of water without her, yet he was so gregarious. He loved her being
near.

I only knew him well in old age but he was not like an old person. He
wasn't nostalgic for the past. He would refer to it to illustrate some
point – just as he might refer to Nero. He had this great ability to live in
the present and to appreciate what was going on. He enjoyed it and

was always curious. Often he discussed Punks and wanted to know how they did their hair and what kept it up.

Without intruding, David could start a conversation immediately. It could alarm strangers used to talking Bradshaws on arrival. He usually wanted to know why this person thought this or that. People became better company as they started to think instead of just coasting. David was not always in happy agreement. Sometimes he would say 'Darling, I think you are talking the most awful nonsense.' This was said totally without malice.

David had a nose for a new book. He was like a truffle hound – he was always successful. When I buy books which is my one real extravagance, I like to savour them, and not feel under any pressure to read them immediately. I used to put them in the nursery but David always found them. His interest in all forms of literature and biography was overwhelming. It was a passion.

David had an adage that 'all the best conversations take place after the dressing gong'.

In his youth there was a convention that you had one amusing neighbour at dinner, and one dull one. David resented this. He wanted two amusing companions.

Both my children when studying for their 'O' Levels had one long tutorial from him, as a result of which Shakespeare became something utterly different. It was no longer an academic subject to be learnt for an exam, but instead it became a revelation of language and a pleasure. They both got top marks.

What I would like to mention was the unbelieveable, really heroic courage shown by David when Rachel was dying. He could not have gone through this without the moral support of the MacMillan nurses. One of them would come and talk to David quite regularly throughout her long illness. He was quite open about not wanting to live after Rachel died. Although his love for his children remained quite unaltered, there was no joy remaining.

He enjoyed mild hypochondria. He once answered when I asked him how he was: 'I'm really very well in myself but I may be going to get a little cold.'

After David's funeral, I was very worried about my sister Elizabeth who had been taken ill the previous evening and had come down for the service. I had no thermometer in the house so I called in at Red Lion House where I asked Laura if she had one. She replied that there were at least twenty thermometers in the house.

One laughed a lot with David and a lot at David but never behind his back. 'David, where did you get that tie?' not 'what an awful tie' when David had gone home.

An Unexpected Friendship

CLARE KIRKMAN

*Clare Kirkman — a friend of David's daughter Laura
and her husband Angelo Hornak. She was taken down
to Red Lion House in the late seventies and immediately
struck up a great friendship with David and Rachel.*

THAT first week-end we sat round the fire in the drawing room, David in his arm-chair, china and small tables in peril at every gesture. Rachel on the sofa, small and alert, an anxious expression on her face as she strained to hear words. I remember we talked a lot about Elizabeth Bowen and her books. Also Barbara Pym, who was to be re-issued. David was very pleased that his piece in the TLS has helped to bring this about.

Over the next two years I used to go and stay with them and once or twice they came to lunch in London. This was not an unalloyed success, since I had underestimated their love of nursery food and had left the new potatoes unpeeled and the vegetables 'al dente'. Later when Rachel became ill, as is natural, their world rather closed in. Laura used to give me news of them though and I went to tea if James and I were near Cranborne.

After Rachel's death, I went to stay again. David often talked about her, gentle and affectionate memories of their life, children and happiness together. At first, on these visits, we used to go and look at churches, Horton Tower, and local manor houses, but as he got older he gave up driving. Since he combined slowness and a complete absence of any road sense this was not entirely a bad thing. Short walks became the order of the day, followed by talk — many people will describe David's conversation better than I; for me it was the pleasure of his interest in and erudite knowledge of such a variety of subjects; books, politics, music, but mainly his fascination and pleasure in people with an enjoyment and understanding of their foibles. This and an ability, the mark of a good teacher, to make his companion feel interesting and intelligent. The conversation would wander from the discussion of a book, to history, politics, opera and then to something totally frivolous, 'which Prime Ministers have had the most sex appeal'. David not surprisingly chose Melbourne, and Harold Wilson.

I wish I could remember in more detail what he said about books. My main memory is of the pleasure he and Rachel got from them, and their ability to share that pleasure. Through him I discovered Barbara Pym, the Misses Findlater, the letters of Harriet Lady Granville, Mrs Oliphant and the later Somerville and Ross. He was surprised that I found P. G. Wodehouse so funny, since he felt it was such a masculine humour, but added that he was influenced by the fact that Rachel had not found Wodehouse amusing.

Every visit I made to David, I was aware that he was becoming physically frailer – more breathless, he tired more eaily, repeated himself now and again, found the cold harder to bear. The last time I stayed there was in November. On the Saturday, we spent a pleasant morning talking, had lunch together and I was expecting him to take his afternoon rest. As usual, he asked what I would like to do, and for some reason I suggested rather tentatively, whether he would like to go for a drive. He leapt at the suggestion and once in the car had a very specific idea of where he wished to go – Cecil Beaton's old house at Broad Chalke, some beech woods, a church and the village where Rachel and he had had a house many years previously. It was a beautiful, bright November afternoon. Though neither of us said anything it needed no great perception on my part to feel that he was aware that it was probably the last autumn for him. It was not sad – his life had been a long and happy one. He died just after Christmas.

David and Music

IONA BROWN

*David derived huge pleasure from music. Friends will remember
how he used to stand in front of the gramophone with his back to
the room, completely and utterly absorbed by what he was
listening to. His love of music was perfectly married to his knowledge
and appreciation of poetry when, on several occasions, he was to
bring the two together in concert – most notably with Iona Brown,
Director of the Academy of St Martin's-in-the-Fields. At what was
to be his last public reading three weeks before he died Iona and
David gave a concert in the Church at Bowerchalke
in aid of the Salisbury Spire Appeal.*

D AVID walked into the church that morning, and I knew instantly
that this would be our last concert together. He had a transparent
look, combined with an air of great serenity. We rehearsed and it was
all great fun. As we worked, people were arranging the flowers and
candles. It was so moving to see David's absolutely professional
approach. He wanted it to be the best, the most perfect evening
possible, so we planned everything very carefully. I would play a
phrase or two and he would say, 'Yes, that's fine, lets do a bit of the
slow movement.'

Although he seemed on one hand terribly excited and enthusiastic –
indeed he would almost go into a dream world whilst listening – he
was also deeply moved by the music. He loved it with a fervour and
respect that are rare.

I can remember waiting in the vestry that evening before we went on.
David was very frail and concentrated, with his papers in front of him,
whilst I tuned my fiddle. He had an amazing air about him. The concert
opened with a carol followed by the organist, Ian Watson, playing a piece
of Bach, after which I played a Handel Sonata. In *Library Looking Glass*
David has mentioned de la Mare on Robert Bridges, 'a balance
between joy and solemnity such as delights and solaces as in the music

[173]

of Handel'. Then David started to read. The church was candle-lit with a spotlight on my music and on his lectern. I can see it now. Suddenly he stopped abruptly, and said, 'Its no good, I've got to come clean − I've brought the wrong spectacles.' It was such a human touch, and so honest, and just saying the truth − everybody adored him for it.

Something similar happened the very first time we gave a concert together with my brother Jan Brown. It was in 1973 and in aid of The British Heart Foundation. David arrived armed with a huge pile of papers. They looked extremely precarious, and, of course, all ended up on the floor just as we were about to start − unnumbered!! Rachel was sitting in the front row and I could see that she was extremely amused.

I still have the programmes for many of the concerts we gave, and they give a good idea of the music he loved the most. After my father's memorial concert, David wrote me a lovely letter reacting to its music, mentioning in particular Vaughan Williams's Lark Ascending which suggested to him the landscape of Wessex and the writings of Hardy. He adored the Andante from the Mozart K 467 Piano Concerto and Bach's B Minor Prelude and Fugue for their serenity and depth.

Sometimes he would come to my concerts, and I particularly remember seeing him at Holkham, where, with my colleagues from the Academy, we were giving a concert in the presence of Queen Elizabeth the Queen Mother. I had to walk down a slippery and quite steep marble staircase in full view of everyone. I was in a long dress, carrying my precious violin with nothing to hold on to. I was absolutely terrified, but, having made it to safety, I sat down and looked along the front row. And there were dear David and Rachel, clapping away and smiling reassuringly. It made all the difference in the world and the performance went beautifully. Afterwards we met for tea with the Queen Mother, and we were all so excited we kept interrupting each other. We had played the Brahms B Flat Sextet, and David was so enthralled by it he couldn't get out the words quickly enough. That afternoon at Holkham he was at his brilliant best − humorous, agitated, and very excited.

The moments in my life spent with David were so precious they will stay with me always. He would often commiserate over the enormous amount of travelling one inevitably has to experience as a musician, and used to say, 'Yes, Jonathan has the same problem but that is the life of an artist − it's *your* life, Iona!'

He had a tremendous intellect, but an even greater heart.

Dorset Country Houses

DAVID BURNETT

David Burnett is the founder of the Dovecote Press. He lives near
Cranborne and became David's companion and driver during
their collaboration over David's last book.

IN 1982 I wrote to David asking if he would be interested in writing
a book on Dorset's country houses, for which I would take the
photographs, act as his chauffeur, and ultimately publish. Looking
back, I marvel at my audacity: we had never met, there was no good
reason for him to be attracted to the idea, and the financial rewards
were certain to be slight. David's reply was hesitant. Rachel was very ill
and he was fearful of leaving her bedside. With typical modesty, he
went on to question his qualifications for tackling a book requiring
detailed knowledge of local history and architecture, but attached to
his reply, almost as if an afterthought, was a list of houses written in his
own idiosyncratic and virtually indecipherable shorthand.

Far from knowing nothing of Dorset's past, what struck me most
forcefully when we eventually met was just how extensive David's
knowledge of the county really was. It was as if through his love of
Thomas Hardy and by living in Dorset for so much of his life he had
absorbed its history and character into his bloodstream. Again and
again when later hunting for a house and hopelessly lost amidst
backwater lanes, he would say, 'I think we turn left here,' and our goal
would emerge into view. He might not have driven those same lanes
for twenty years, but their imprint endured in his unconscious. Hardly
a house we discussed was unfamiliar to him. Many of their owners
were friends. Perhaps most importantly he had visited virtually all the
houses on his list before, some as much as fifty years earlier, and had
known them in more spacious days, before war and social change had
reduced their households and revenue.

Despite David's reluctance to fully commit himself, there were some houses he wanted to look at again and we agreed on a series of 'recces'. Three days of memorable trespassing followed. We criss-crossed Dorset, boldly motoring up drives and peering over hedges. Occasionally we were compelled to be even more resolute, warily watching for game keepers as we ducked through undergrowth in order to inspect this or that facade. David made light of the hazards. 'I don't think I look like a poacher', he insisted. I was less certain. His cap and scarf invoked a rakish almost roguish air.

In between such forays we talked incessantly; about the houses, their virtues and defects, and of the families who had lived in them. But also about books and literature, and Dorset itself. David moved from one subject to the next with a speed that left me floundering. Ideas seemed to spring fully-formed into his mind. I have never met anyone who wore his wisdom and learning so lightly. He never preached or talked down, but seemed instinctively to understand when I was out of my depth and needed prompting or guidance. Of course there were silences, when I sensed his thoughts were with Rachel, or of a time when the two of them had driven the same route together – on the way to friends, or for a picnic on the open downland that David so delighted in. When he finally started the book I gradually came to perceive that part of its appeal lay in this sense of retracing his steps to places he had been to with Rachel, or of journeys once shared with her through the countryside he knew and loved best.

Rachel's illness grew steadily worse. The prospect of beginning any book was set aside and not picked up for nearly a year, by which time Rachel had died. One day the phone rang. It was David, eager to begin and with his letters to the owners of the houses he wanted to include already written and answered.

We started at once, I thought inauspiciously, for when pausing in Blandford I reversed into another car whilst parking. 'Don't worry,' said David, cheerfully waving me forward, 'I'm always bumping into cars.' Only later, when he insisted on driving me to Sixpenny Handley, did I realise how plausible was his confession.

My memories of the two years that followed remain as bright as ever. For the sake of David's health we restricted our house visits to spring and summer, and never before or since have I so longed for the winters to end. April to August meant being in his company at least once a week, usually Wednesdays. We met at Red Lion House, often returning to retrieve a forgotten notepad or coat. Then we drove to the house we were visiting that day, curious as to what lay ahead, occasionally slowing to savour the glorious riches of landscape and vista that only Dorset at its most lovely can offer.

David had selected about thirty houses for possible inclusion in what he was determined to make a very personal choice of the county's country houses, intending finally to prune their numbers to nearer twenty. A childhood spent partly at Cranborne Manor cast its spell over his choice, for by instinct he was drawn to the smaller manor houses, with their more domestic atmosphere, their more intimate relationship with the surrounding countryside. Yet, as always with David, people took precedence over buildings. How could he omit a castle if Raleigh had once lived in it, or a stately home if built by Vanbrugh for Bubb Dodington?

What I am sure David had not counted on when making his selection were the welcomes that awaited us on arrival. At the first house we visited poor David was greeted as 'Lord Cecil' and persuaded to begin his tour of inspection bent double amidst the boiler piping that filled the cellar. Two hours later, his notepad firmly back in his pocket, he was led out in triumph onto the roof by an owner who had barely drawn breath from the moment we walked through the door. Worse was still to come. Once downstairs again David was ushered ceremoniously into the drawing room to find thirty complete strangers had been invited to meet him over tea. David was normally extraordinarily tolerant on such occasions, but the prospect ahead was more than he could bear. An excuse was hastily invented and we started to retreat. Never will I forget the look of mixed horror and disbelief on the face of our hostess as David shook hands with her maid at the door, apologizing for having to leave so suddenly and congratulating her on owning so charming a house, whilst the other guests watched from the doorway. Even David was silent as we drove away, but finally he said, 'I think they must have got the wrong Cecil.'

Nor indeed will I forget him sitting, fully dressed and knees hunched, in an otherwise empty bath whilst the owner of another house we visited pressed a button that revealed a television set in the wall above the taps. No expense had been spared when doing it up, hence the insistence that David sit in one of the ten bathrooms that partnered the ten guest bedrooms. Once again it was a house that fell at an early fence, mainly I suspect because of David's aversion to the white pile carpet that covered every flag and oak floorboard in what was

[177]

an exquisite Georgian house. David said it made him feel like an eskimo.

Lunch twice led to incidents that upset David greatly. At the first our host became so sozzled he collapsed onto his sideplate during pudding, thereafter occasionally lifting his head to blame taxation and the incumbent Prime Minister for his woes. David and I sat in bewildered silence until a sympathetic butler, obviously used to such lapses, quietly led his employer from the room.

The other incident was less upsetting to David, who was an old friend of our first host. We were lunching in some style, but the arrival of a decanter of port to go with the cheese finally made it quite clear to both of us that neither our host or hostess were going to be able to fulfill their promise to take us round the house after lunch. Happily, they also sensed the disaster ahead. A retainer was summoned to take their places, and much later in the afternoon we came across them both fast asleep on sofas in a small upstairs sitting room.

Such incidents were as rare as they were invigorating. More often than not we were welcomed in the most friendly way, given lunch, taken on tours of both house and grounds, and sent homeward for Cranborne with David tired but content. I soon noticed that the shabbier and more lived in the house the greater its appeal to him. Ensconced in a comfortable armchair in a drawing room piled with books and surrounded by possessions accumulated over centuries he visibly relaxed. His gestures became more erratic, his words faster, the angle of his sherry glass gradually more acute as the hand holding it fell further over the arm of his chair. A leg might kick impatiently if he grew eager to end a conversation and begin looking round the house. His notepad was his biggest foe, for he was always putting it down and then forgetting it, which in turn meant having to send out search parties. Because what he wrote in it was illegible to me, its contents remained a mystery from the moment he embarked on the book to its conclusion.

Some of the owners, unfamiliar with David's ways, were I think disconcerted by the speed at which he inspected their properties. He took in long gallerys and great halls at a glance. Paintings of distinguished forbears were examined in seconds. Entire herbaceous borders were admired in the time it took him to walk their length. Once he had found his bearings it was he who led, and at times it was impossible to believe he was in his eighties. If it was a hot day or there were lots of stairs he became out of breath, and would pause to gather his strength. Occasionally he deliberately slowed down, withdrawing himself from his escort, to gaze in silence at the outside of a house. In retrospect I realize that at such moments he was searching for pegs on which to hang his words – absorbing the atmosphere of the house, its character and mood.

More obvious from the outset was David's sense of kinship with many of the owners, particularly if, like the Cecils and Cranborne, the same family had lived in a house for centuries. There was time for gossip, for news of mutual friends. The conversations at lunch were then a delight. David's wit and keen intelligence predominated, but in such a way that he always made the rest of us seem cleverer than we really were. He openly admired the resilience of the owners, their ability to adapt to their changing fortunes, their apparent indifference to the cold which pervaded many of the larger houses, even in summer. But at times, on seeing yet another wing shut up or the lady of the house rise from weeding to greet us, he wistfully recalled an age which he knew was over and would never return.

Some Dorset Country Houses was published in November 1985, a bare two months before David's death. Yet right to the end he rang almost daily to offer advice and ask how the book was doing. Such concern was unnecessary, for it sold out by Christmas and has since been twice reprinted.

David deliberately delayed our visit to Cranborne Manor until every other house had been written up. He knew it would be easy to write, and only insisted we go round it out of kindness to me. It was high summer, the gardens were closed and the house empty. Walking through its rooms he recalled his childhood. At the top of the stairs leading upward from the hall he knelt behind the front of the gallery to show me how as a boy he had crept from his bedroom to eavesdrop on the dinner guests below. Suddenly his head popped up. He was grinning contentedly, and on his face was all the vigour and innocence of boyhood. It was how I will always remember him.

David's Religion

GERARD IRVINE

*Gerard Irvine is Prebendary Emeritus of St Paul's
and a long standing family friend.*

I FIRST got to know David at Oxford during the war, though, since I was not reading English, I only sat under him for the occasional lecture. As a notable Oxford 'personality', acquaintance with him was sought after by many; amongst others by me. Partly, no doubt, out of intellectual and social snobbery; but also for a less discreditable reason. While still at school I had read *The Stricken Deer*. Already a fervent Anglocatholic, in full adolescent revolt against the Protestant *ethos* of the school, and the dominant humanism of the highbrow circles which in other respects I admired, the imaginative sympathy shown in this book for Cowper's sufferings at the hands of what seemed to me then (and still seems) an appalling travesty of the Gospel, had profoundly moved me; and I felt the author must be someone whose outlook accorded with mine. So when at Oxford I found that my sister's digs in Savile House were next to where the Cecils were then living, I jumped at the chance thus afforded of getting to know them. As David and Rachel were always generous to the young, the hospitality of their home was soon extended to me.

After Oxford I had little chance of seeing them until the middle sixties, when Jonathan came to live in my parish in Earls Court as a student at LAMDA, a drama school of which I was then chaplain. Through him my friendship with the family revived; and thereafter it grew steadily. At the time of Rachel's death, I was privileged to be of some little use to David as a spiritual consellor.

As I look back, I do not remember him ever talking much about his religion, odd though this may seem for so extrovert, voluble and uninhibited a conversationalist, gifted with a critical and acute mind, and enjoying argument and the exchange of ideas. Not that he was irreligious, or indifferent to spiritual issues. Far from it: he was a devout and orthodox believer with an *anima naturaliter anglicana*. Rather I think that for him God was not one subject among many others in which he was interested, but the pervasive centre of his whole life, giving meaning and value to everything else.

Though not by temperament or training a philosopher, his outlook was platonic, in that he saw in the visible world a reflexion of spiritual reality, from which, and for which, we are created. This attitude he spelt out in an address given at St James's Church Piccadilly in 1978 on *the Value of Literature*

We are divided, we are born with a soul that derives from a spiritual region and partakes of its nature, which is a desire for perfection. But we are born into a fallen world, a sinful world which is imperfect, limited, flawed, disappointing. The result is that the soul isn't at home, not really at home in this world. Now what art does is to give us an image of perfection which softens the soul's longing. It gives a glimpse of the world unfallen, and by so doing it nourishes and strengthens and inspires us . . . Great art draws its power from what is the first Source of spiritual life, the first and final Source. And it reveals a profounder reality than we see in this world, that is apparent on this imperfect earth. Shakespeare's vision – it isn't only more beautiful than that we see, it's truer, it's deeper. And the perfection it shows us is not a dream, a daydream or a delusion, it is something that lives more intensely than anything in the transient world we know.

This platonic outlook, while independent of any particular articulation of belief seems to come naturally to those whose temperaments are of the type categorized by William James as 'once-born'. In his classic study *The Varieties of Religious Experience* the characteristics of the once-born type are thus described

They see God not as a strict Judge, not a Glorious Potentate; but as the animating Spirit of a beautiful harmonious world, beneficent and kind, merciful as well as pure. The same characters generally have no metaphysical tendencies: they do not look back into themselves. Hence they are not distressed by their own imperfections; yet it would be absurd to call them self-righteous; for they hardly think of themselves at all. . . they have no vivid conception of *any* of the qualities in which the severer Majesty of God consists. He is to them the impersonation of kindness and beauty. They read his character not in the disordered world of man, but in romantic and harmonious nature. Of human sin they know perhaps little in their own hearts and not very much in the world, and human suffering does but melt them to tenderness. Thus when they approach God, no human disturbance ensues.

Discounting the rather unsophisticated style, which perhaps says more about the writer than the subject, this description of the once-born temperament surely fits David. He used to claim that his life had been exceptionally happy, both in the external circumstances of family background, education, work and (above all) a supremely happy marriage; in the pleasure which he saw as the chief of purpose of art, together with the enjoyment of the two things which he used to say never palled, landscape and friendship. To these blessings we can add the particular gift of his own charming, debonair personality.

This happiness was reflected in his religion. Not for him the torments – or the ecstasy – of the 'twice-born' man, the spiritual side of whose nature coexists in (often agonising) tension, or alternation with a secular side. To such men – and their number includes some of the greatest saints – the religious capacity can be submerged, even unknown, until in an identifiable experience of conversion, Grace bears down upon them so overwhelmingly as to transform their lives, with a conviction that this alone is that 'new birth' without which no one can enter the Kingdom of God.

David, I am sure, never had an evangelical conversion of this sort. It would have been something incompatible with his whole nature. To him the essential new birth was something which had happened in his unremembered infancy, at his christening. He was conscious of sin, and of the call to holiness; but he was not haunted by guilt. For him glory and adoration, rather than liberation from sin, was at the deep heart of his spirituality.

A temptation to which the 'once-born' soul is especially prone is to be so caught by the beauty of the Gospel as to pay scant regard to its moral claims. To this temptation he did not succumb. His ethical standards were firm and traditional, not least in matters of sexual morality. In a letter discussing Graham Greene's *The Heart of the Matter*, whose hero, Scobie, having committed adultery from motives of compassion, commits suicide and so 'dies in mortal sin', leaving open to the reader the question of his final salvation, David commented critically: 'If Almighty God is good, he will forgive Scobie, given that his sinful acts were really activated by Christian love of his fellows, and not just a warm, self-indulgent emotion, projected on to others. Of course if they are in fact activated by this last, they are much less likely to be forgiven – and don't deserve to be.' He then typically adds: 'But I should not trespass on to this theological territory, where you know much more than I do. Anyway I am not a very strict moralist, and feel a humbug about taking a strict line.' In fact he was the least judgemental of men.

His moral and spiritual life was a process of gradual deepening, not a sudden transformation. He admitted that he once – perhaps only once: we do not know – had a profound religious experience. Its form and content can only be a matter of speculation. Possibly it was similar to that vouchsafed to his grandfather, the Prime Minister Lord Salisbury, of which he writes in *The Cecils of Hatfield House*:

Some time before he was out of his teens he underwent a momentous spiritual experience. What form it took no one knows, for he never said. But his daughter Gwendolen, who knew him better than anyone else, thought it involved an intimate sense of what he believed to be the living and personal presence of Christ. This experience was so overwhelming that it became the foundation of a faith which was to endure unshaken until death, and it conditioned his permanent and basic attitude to life.

Certainly David's piety was unambiguously Christian, and indeed Christocentric. But it also involved a basically Catholic sense of the centrality of the Church. For him devotion was never 'the flight of the alone to the alone', but an activity involving participation in a worshipping community, most fully expressed in liturgy and the sacramental life. By tradition and temperament a sacramentalist, he found inward grace primarily through outward and visible – and audible – signs. Words and music were for him the prime vehicles of truth in religious as in secular affairs. His distaste for the *Alternative Service Book*, an aversion he shared with other members of his family, was not just a matter of aesthetic or purely conservative preference for traditional usage. It was because he believed that words ultimately *matter*, new and banal words are signs of new and inferior meaning. Whenever possible he would attend services which followed the language of the Book of Common Prayer; but when he could not, he was quite prepared to attend those of the new ASB, if that was the rite followed by the local congregation. This he did from loyalty to his profound belief that worship was a corporate activity of the Church and not just an act of individual piety.

Inevitably his own religious formation was firmly Anglican, as befitted a descendant of Lord Burleigh, who may be said to have *invented* the Church of England (at least as an autonomous body), and an inheritor of the tradition of his immediate forebears, exemplified by his grandfather and his Uncles, 'Fish', (Lord William Cecil, the holy and eccentric Bishop of Exeter), Robert (Lord Cecil of Chelwood) and, most notably, Hugh (Lord Quickswood) all luminaries of the High Church tradition. But, unlike the uncles, he was little concerned with church politics or parties. Though by no means a 'paid-up Anglocatholic', he found his instinct for tradition and his devotional sensibilities most fully satisfied in the catholic wing of the Church of England. When the family moved to North Oxford, in addition to his College chapel, and the Cathedrals, he frequented St Mary Magdalene's, arguably the 'highest' church in the city, in preference to the very evangelical church down the road. Partly this choice may have been due to the Vicar, Fr. Colin Stephenson with whom the whole family developed a warm friendship; partly because his children found the worship there more interesting than elsewhere; and partly because of Rachel, who, brought up in the inner circles of Bloomsbury in which all religion was held to be absurd, and finding her own way into the Church, was prepared to go much further than David in the Catholic direction. Indeed after her death he was inclined to accuse himself that it was only his entrenched Anglicanism that prevented him from becoming a Roman Catholic.

Whether or not he was justified in this, I don't know. What is quite evident is that their marriage was as nearly perfect a union as is granted to humans; and her death in 1982 was a shattering blow to him. But though his life may have been shattered, his faith was not. At the time of her death he wrote in a letter 'I deeply believe that Rachel is only dead in the sense that she is not now physically with me'. And a year later: 'I do so deeply believe that her spirit lives and is aware of mine, and I should like to think that my consciousness of this was signalised, as it were sacramentally, by a Requiem ... Strangely enough I have not been very unhappy. God must have helped me. But of course, I do miss her – not surprisingly after 50 years of supremely happy marriage'.

A Requiem was duly said, and in a letter of thanks he wrote that it 'was all I could have wished and hoped for; beautiful, personal and hopeful', and added 'I responded to it all the more because now that Rachel has been dead nearly a year, I find myself – not all the time, but sometimes – in a strange state, missing her perhaps more than before, but in a dumb, dull sort of way, but somehow lifelessly and finding it harder to find her still living. The service brought her personality back and alive to me, rousing a sort of tender, quiet, happy acceptance of her as still alive and aware of me'.

Writing after another Year's Mind Requiem two years later: 'I can't quite believe that Rachel has been dead three years; it seems only a few months. And yet it also seems a long time since I saw her and I miss her more than I did, and yet at moments feel her far away, so that the Requiem and you speaking of her – and I loved what you said – was a reminder of her presence. Thank you.'

In one of these letters, dated shortly after Rachel's death, asking that I should pray for him as well as for her, he had written: 'I am not a strong spirit and will be in need of prayers'. That he, like us all, needed prayers is certain; but in this assessment of insufficient strength he characteristically underrated himself. His was not indeed the naturally *robust* spirit of such friends and contemporaries as C. S. Lewis, Sir Isaiah Berlin or Maurice Bowra. But he had a full measure of fortitude, that gift of the Spirit rising from a tranquil faith, which is manifest not least in the lives of the courteous and gentle-hearted.

Acknowledgements

I must thank all those friends who have made full contributions to the book, but I am equally indebted to the many others whose anecdotes and recollections have helped bring this portrait of David Cecil to life.

I should also like to thank the following for generously allowing the inclusion of their photographs: Dr Hugh Cecil, Mrs Frances Partridge, The Marquess of Salisbury, The Earl of Snowdon, Mrs Janet Stone, Lady Anne Tree, The Trustees of the Cecil Beaton Estate.

I am also in debt to the BBC for allowing me to publish part of the transcript from the interview 'Conversations at Cranborne', Miss Norah Hartley for the introduction to David Cecil's 'Festschrift', Ludovic Kennedy and his publishers, Collins, for an extract from *On my Way to the Club*, the Royal Society of Literature for Sir Isaiah Berlin's obituary of David Cecil, Mrs George Scott for an extract from *A Time and Place* by George Scott (Staples Press 1956) and *The Wadham Gazette* for Sir Henry Phelps Brown's obituary of David Cecil. To all the above and countless others who I have failed to mention, I am deeply grateful.

HANNAH CRANBORNE

Books published